MY LIFE A TESTAMENT OF STRENGTH:
How to Triumph While Waiting

BEVERLY ANN DAVIS

JWG Publishing

Dedication

Dedicated to my father Leroy Davis who passed in 2008,
and my brother Kelvin Davis who passed in 2018.
You will never be forgotten.

ISBN: 978-1-7353610-5-5

Unless otherwise expressed, all quotations and references must
be permitted by Authors. All scripture references from NKJ
and NIV Bibles.

Cover Design:
Business Startup & Marketing Solutions LLC
and JWG Publishing House.

Published by

JWG Publishing
Printed in the United States of America.

TABLE OF CONTENTS

INTRODUCTION

This book will provide real-life situations and thought processes that led me to a better understanding of what my purpose is. It will show you how to overcome the negative effects of childhood traumas, misguided intentions, and character-building flaws. Although everyone may be impacted differently, this book should help to provoke an awakening of areas, emotions, and decisions that were not properly addressed or were repressed altogether. You will read through a series of events that occurred in different areas of my life that will show practical, mental, and spiritual growth now, which I once mismanaged because of a lack of knowing my true identity. You will read about a young mother, a girl who once considered her voice to not be heard by others in authority, her household, and the very situations that tried to define her. Through the branding of other people's negative interpretation of her life, she found her voice. I will share the effects of work situations I encountered in the most difficult times, and results that led to better understandings and triumph in life. You will also read about my transition to a more spiritually awakened state, a calling to the ministry, deeper revelations, and the manifestation of God's love toward me and others.

You will encounter a mother's love for her child and a child's love for her mother in return, which led to therapy later in her adulthood. You will read about an adolescent trying to figure out her way in a big world, which led to drug use, alcoholism, sexual promiscuity, and rejection. There were also later events that I encountered as a single parent with limited income that created unimaginable issues for both me and my daughter, that negatively affected the home. You will learn how my professional and educational awareness began and how it improved over time, leading to better outcomes socially and financially: growing from deficiency to entrepreneurship, working with a government agency, and becoming a leader in the church. None of the information stated in this book is intended to shift blame to others or justify my actions. This book is solely meant to highlight how my thought process was framed then, and how my actions were reciprocated accordingly.

Chapter 1

THE FAMILY DYNAMIC

The day I found out that I was pregnant was a very emotional, scary, and frightening one. I had babysat so many of my siblings' children, taking care of them from the toddler stage up to school age. That still had not prepared me for the reality of pregnancy. I didn't know what my mother would say, or how she would react. My mother was a very strong woman, and a religious one. She was Pentecostal, so for me to engage in pre-marital sex was a big deal, and not a good one.

I knew this would be hard for my mother to deal with; she was a leader in the church. When I heard about the backlash she encountered, it was troubling. As a mother, it was hard for her, but I know as a parent she wanted the best for her children like I now want for my child. Yes, back then, during those times, my mother would always tell us God was talking to her. God is telling her this and that, but I often thought it was a myth. I wasn't spiritually connected like I am now, but I was raised to be. Sometimes I would be frightened by what she said, but I did not show it externally because I did not want to show any signs of weakness and disbelief. My mother had always demonstrated strength in front of us and showed us you can get through anything, believing and trusting in God. When situations became challenging in my mother's life, I never saw her break down; instead, she went down in prayer. Her tears were always followed by prayer.

So that illustrated to me that, even though being pregnant was difficult, even though it was frightening, I should keep going. And that is the mindset I held on to as I tried to figure things out. I did not seek help from any of my siblings because it was a challenging time for the family. I did not even know what to say and how to say it. I eventually ended up going to

10

my friend's mother, Ms. Darlene, for help. I knew I needed to get some help because my child's father was not in the picture. I had gotten involved with him in my late teens and became pregnant. With Ms. Darlene's help in allowing me to use her address to receive public assistance, I was able to handle some things of my own, which made it easier for me to deal with my situation. I could not let my mother know that I was getting assistance; I could not use her address because my other siblings were using it for the same reason. So I had to use Ms. Darlene's. I did this primarily because I did not tell my mother I was pregnant. So, imagine my surprise when my mother confronted me and asked me, "Are you pregnant?" I did not hide it; I told her yes and that I had already spoken to Ms. Darlene and told her my situation: that I needed an income and I needed to use her address for welfare. This was how I started life with my daughter, on welfare.

I did not know what it took to be a mother other than what I saw in my home and around me. I did not know about the emotional journey it would take me on. I did not know that babies could touch you to your core; I didn't know it was the place where selfishness is eliminated, because mothers do not make decisions for themselves only but for the betterment of their child. I did not know these things because I was still a child. I was in my late teens, but a teen nevertheless; I was the baby of the family. Everybody else was grown; they knew life and could tell me about it, but it was my responsibility to figure things out on my own.

Although I was primarily raised in a two-parent home, my father was not around most times, but I did not understand why because I was young. My older siblings understood more than I did, but I loved my father very much. I felt like he was the best thing since sliced bread, and because he was more easy-going than my mother, I gravitated to him more. I remember times when my dad would sit and talk with me; he would ask me about how my day was going and things like that. I would tell him things that were going on with me, and how I was feeling. He would take his time to tell me, "Well, you know what? You can do it this way or that way." My father was my only outlet. He was my confidante; I could release to him and he always knew what to say. That was how I released when I experienced tough times with others because I was not being heard by others. Not being heard would frustrate me, and that frustration would turn to anger, and that anger came out through fighting.

I was known as a fighter because I could not communicate my pain or annoyance. Even when I verbally communicated, I wouldn't be heard because of my type of communication. One of my favorite memories of my father when he was around, was when he would take me and my siblings during the holidays to the Cheltenham Mall to see the holiday lights. We would take pictures with Santa Claus and go shopping. We had fun. I have fond memories sometimes of dad being home and my mother would have the center table out with the younger kids sitting around it and the other table had everyone else congregating. My mom would be sewing, and my dad would be eating.

My dad would eat very weird stuff. He would make up strange concoctions of food to eat. I remembered those joyous moments and how my dad would get up from the table and would say to my mom, "Come on," and my mother would respond, "All right, crazy." He would grab her and start slow dancing with her, and we would all laugh. I remember those moments just as much as when my father was not around. So, in my mind, I attributed moments of happiness and joy to only be present when my father was present. Especially because that was the only time that I felt that I was seen, heard, and understood. I did not have that anywhere else. I didn't have people to help me construct those areas of my life growing up. Remember, everyone was older and concerned with their own thing. My siblings were in relationships; they were living their lives. In my young mind, I felt they only needed me when they needed a babysitter; I didn't hear from them otherwise. Everybody was just in

13

their own world.

When I found out that my dad and my mom had separated, it was extremely hard for me, because no one took the time to tell me that this had happened. I came home one day and was told, "Daddy doesn't live here anymore." That was it. I did not and could not understand it. No one explained why, or what happened. It just was the way it was going to be. My new normal. That experience brought on a new set of challenges. So even after I had my baby, my family could not understand why I couldn't communicate without anger; they had no clue that the hurt and frustration I felt towards my family had to do with my father leaving unannounced. I was closer to one of my siblings more than the others; it was our relationship that helped me to begin the healing process.

I recall being on the basketball team while I was at Job Corps and one day we had a team game off-site, which meant we had to travel by bus. I remember those in charge telling us as we got on the bus not to wear certain colors, because they had to drive through the gang-infested neighborhoods, to get to the final location. I remember making up my mind at that point that I wanted to go home, but just as I had that thought, gang members began to shoot at the bus, we had to duck downwards. As the driver drove his hardest to get us out of there, it was a frightening experience.

That was a close call, but God shielded us. Because although they were shooting at the bus, when we got off the bus, there were no bullet holes in the bus. Now back then, as a child, the ordeal I had just gone through didn't register. I quickly packed up everything that I had, I was ready to go home; I knew I wasn't going to go back there. Leaving Job Corps wasn't easy: In order to be sent home you had to make the staff believe that you got in trouble and you didn't want to go home, at which point they would simply put you in a separate section at the facility away from everyone. But I wanted to go home for good. I was past the age requirement for the school district to go after my mother for truancy.

I knew she wouldn't get in trouble for me going home, and I knew I was not going to go back. So, when they finally sent me home, and my mom would ask me, "Are you going back?" I quickly told her, "Mom, I am not going back to that place." I never told her what happened, or what transpired on that fateful day. I was just determined that I was never going back to that place. After returning home for good, I got with my daughter's father and became pregnant.

Chapter 2

WHERE WORK BEGAN

In chapters 2 and 3 I will take you on a journey. I will go back and forth addressing the middle of my journey, my early years, with a peep into the present, before closing out. Buckle up!

I will share that I have been in the healthcare industry for a while. I stumbled upon healthcare when I had my child in February 1997. By then, I was a single parent. My child's father was not actively around by choice. I knew that I could not raise her on my own and had realized that I had gotten myself into something bigger than I could handle. I will never forget the first time I looked at her face; she had the most beautiful, big brown eyes. I was so overprotective of her and wanted to do everything right by her. I wanted to protect her with my all and give her all the love I could give. I was a young adult by now; I was then 20, and still did not know much about hardships. As mentioned earlier, before becoming pregnant, I lived at home with my mother. I did not have to pay bills or have many responsibilities except for listening to my mother, attending church, cleaning, cooking (if I had to), and looking after my nieces and nephews. I did not have big responsibilities or adult issues.

Though having a baby made me feel like I had gotten into something bigger than I could handle. I remembered God and the promise I made Him, laying looking at my baby's face. "God, if You help me to raise this baby, I will give her back to You. Help me to raise her right, like I was raised in the church, according to Your Word, and I will give her back to You." At the time I did not realize the magnitude of what I was saying, but I knew that this was the right thing to do. Although my teenage and adolescent years may have been challenging for both my mother and me while growing up, I never forgot the Word of God or the prayers that my mother prayed, or the church services I had attended. The church was a safe haven for me. So I wanted my child to be placed in that haven too, committed and contracted back to God.

I knew I had to get a job to take care of my baby even if I had to work 10 jobs and that I almost did. I worked at a recreation center during the summer, before being pregnant. Shortly after, I worked a temp job at a very prestigious office in the Spring Garden section of Philadelphia. Though I cannot recall the type of business, I can remember everyone in that establishment had an uppity attitude, and I just thought, wow. I managed to earn my GED and a diploma from Temple University. I needed welfare and at that time, the Department of Welfare was only willing to give me $105.50.

I made several sacrifices so that even before my daughter was born, she had everything she needed, as did any child with two parents who had larger incomes and a more stable life. I knew my daughter was special, so whether I had clothes, food, or shelter for myself or not, my baby would. By the time she finally came, she changed my entire world. I knew making a better life for her would require me to do and be better; I had to complete school and get my diploma. Two of my other siblings were also attending Temple University for their diplomas and other programs too. They did this so that they could continue their childcare, which was fully funded for a student, but I was actually attending to better myself so that I could live a better life for myself and my child.

Attending school was a lot harder than I thought it would be, but the teachers and the program directors saw my dedication, that I was really trying to fairly obtain my diploma. Oh, it was such a struggle! They could see it. One day a young man came over to me and said, "Hey I want to introduce myself to you. I want you to sit in on this program that we are doing called medical billing and coding. I think you would like it." I told him I would sit in on one of the classes just to see what it was about. I did, and it instantly grabbed my attention. It was very interesting, and I wanted to learn more about it. The young man who invited me to the class told me that if I liked it, I should let my caseworker know. I was excited. However, when I went back to my caseworker at the public assistance office to inform her of my interest in the class, she told me that would not be possible because I could only receive benefits and compensation for one program at a time. I was unhappy because I could not afford it on my own, and my public assistance income was not enough to cover it. They were only willing to fund the diploma at that time, but I kept persisting. I would ask people for copies of their books and notes, and this is how I was able to study medical billing and coding on my own.

I completed the course as if I were really in this class. I

ended up going to take my high school equivalency diploma test at the Community College of Philadelphia (CCP). While I was there, one of the directors of the program came to me and stated they noticed that they did not receive any funding for me for the billing and coding class. I had to tell them the truth about my love for the program and how I maneuvered studying the course along with preparing for my diploma. I will never forget the director's response. He said, "Beverly, you have shown so much dedication and perseverance, more than the people who were receiving the funds to attend, and you never missed a class. You turn in work on time and if you had come to us sooner, maybe we could have done something, tried to figure some things out, but because you showed this persistency and commitment, when you didn't have to, we're going to sponsor you in this class." That is how I ended up getting the award for finishing. I got recognition for both my high school equivalency diploma and the medical billing and coding class.

I finally received my diploma and was now able to transition from public welfare to a work life. I'm glad I did because when I was on welfare, I was on for 18 months and I remember I went to ask if there was any way I could qualify for more money. My caseworker said to me, "You need to have another child, if you want more money; the income is based on family sizes." Needless to say, I was already determined to get off of public assistance, so her advice was not what I wanted to hear. Soon after, I landed my first job assignment with NovaCare's central billing office.

I had to report to my caseworker that I had gotten a job, and when I did, I was immediately cut off from the system, before I even got my first paycheck. Because they cut me off so quickly, things began to become a little tight. Remember, my daughter was a toddler, and I did not have a lot, nor did I have strong family support to help me with my baby. My family was a divided one, though it is a large one, I'm the last of fourteen children. I had to deal with not having emotional or physical support. I told myself this will either break me or make me, but I knew I had to keep going on for the sake of my child. My daughter gave me the drive and motivation to keep going. It was hard for us many times, but I kept going.

Working at NovaCare was God sent at that moment in time. They were known for their sports therapy, occupational, speech, and physical therapy; my job was to take care of motor vehicle accident billing and therapies. It was tough juggling everything: I was a 21-year-old and was dealing with a lot of emotions and work stress, but that job forced me to grow up. I took a lot of bruises, went through a lot of character building, a lot of hurts, and a lot of pain. I got disrespected many times, I even got accused of sexual harassment by a guy! I had finally gotten a car and would help him because he always walked to work. One day I asked him for money to help with gas, and he went to HR and accused me of sexual harassment. Isn't that crazy?

I learned so much from that situation. There were other people that I was connected with that I thought were friends, but I found out they weren't. These experiences gave me the grounding that I needed for the workforce and taught me how to deal with some uncomfortable situations. I will never forget when I was leaving the job, I was basically threatened because they were upset that I was leaving. Needless to say, I left and in 2011, I got a position as a billing clerk at Einstein Healthcare Network in the billing office. I was there for nine years.

I got that job because a friend of mine who also worked at NovaCare left and went to Einstein, and she told me she was going to help me get hired at Einstein too, so when a position became available, I was there in no time for an interview. My girlfriend had so much confidence in me she would say, "I know you can do it. I know you will nail it." I was so ready to leave Valley Forge, PA, and work closer to home because it was so time-consuming, traveling to Valley Forge, and driving back every day on the I-76. Yet I was still thankful to have a car to drive, because taking the bus was not convenient, but the commute time added to the time taken away from being with my child. I remember the day I got my car; it was one day before leaving NovaCare. I met a woman who had a four-door Buick that she was selling for $800. She said she was selling the car because she hit a deer, and she no longer wanted the car, and so I bought the car. I no longer had to catch any more buses. Now I had a car, and I had the means to get around more, but I had to get car insurance; even though it was a relief from the bus transportation, it brought on additional costs.

I had a sibling who told me it was hard for her family and her husband to get to work. They needed a means of transport because they did not have a way to get around. She further stated that her husband had started a new job, and he needed to get back and forth to work and they did not have the money to do so. They had children and they were struggling. She asked if they could borrow my car, and, though I really did not want to lend it to them, I was reminded that I had told God that when He blessed me with a car that I would help as many people as I could. Accordingly, I said, "Okay, when I come home from work, I will lend you the car, but please let me have it back in the morning before I have to leave for work." Well, I found out later that her husband was robbing people with my car and almost got caught carrying out a robbery, when he ran and left my car, and the police confiscated it. I was livid. I threatened to beat up everyone and get him arrested if they did not get my car back. They returned my car to me by the end of the week.

When I left NovaCare for Ameri-Choice, I only stayed for a week because I was offered a full-time job at Einstein's billing office, and things began to get better for me. This was a relief for me and my child. This is also when I began to work on structuring and building my communication skills, personality traits, and every character attribute I needed to build.

I ended up struggling again because of my personality. I never grasped the principle of working with others, especially working with such a diverse set of people, because I was forced into a lot of growing situations. I was young, and when I got upset on the job I would act like the young, immature girl I was. I did not know how to act professionally, being a parent "forced" me into the situation to grow up, but I was still learning what that meant. I knew I had to do whatever it took to keep my job in order to provide for my daughter, so as I worked on myself, I picked up a few odd jobs. I worked at KFC at one point, and also at PNC Bank. While taking up these extra jobs and getting extra funds was necessary and helpful, it took a lot of time from my daughter – the time that should be spent with her, because while I was working, she would be in daycare, then after-school care. This brought on another dilemma because the money that I was making was basically going back into childcare. After all, I did not have anyone to watch her.

After my nine-years' stint, I got another job at Einstein Network's main campus, as a billing coordinator in the gastroenterology department. I had now been at Einstein for 17 years, and I started to feel unfulfilled. The company had gone through several changes and layoffs, which had me worried because I wanted to go back to school; not having a degree made me a prime candidate to be laid off as well. This was when I decided I needed to set specific goals for myself, like completing my degree by a certain time. My ultimate goal was to have my PhD in public health before age 50. I had just graduated from Thomas Jefferson University in Philadelphia, in 2018, with a bachelor's in health services management. I worked hard to achieve this. I went to night school and took extra classes at Einstein campus, some at the Godfrey campus, and others at the main campus. I worked throughout the time that I took these classes. I am now able to do it because my daughter is in college herself. The transition from parent to student was hard because my life had been so centered around my child that I did not even know what I liked to eat at one point. I had to pray to God and ask Him to give me a sense of direction on where to go. And He told me it was time to do it; He reminded me that the reason I wanted to get a degree was to help my daughter financially, also because I knew she was going to be needing that support.

Despite my educational wins, I felt like I was supposed to be doing more in the community. I felt the job I was doing was mediocre and routine. I loved helping people to understand the importance of health insurance and how to use it for their health needs. But I got to a place where I did not care how I looked because it felt like no one saw or heard me. It was like I was invisible. This reflected on my self-worth and how I perceived and felt about myself; I was not taking care of myself. I just had this mentality of "who cares, if I do not care?" I couldn't shake off this mentality, even after I graduated, and that was something major that I should have celebrated. I felt it was not a big deal. I was used to people downplaying my accomplishments, so it became common for me not to celebrate good things in my life because I had no one around to celebrate them with. To be at my current level of achievement at this age is nothing but the grace of God, and I thank Him daily because He gave me the will to finish. Before this, there were so many things that I started but could not seem to finish. I had so many big ideas; graduating college was one, and I was seeing the finish line, but it was God who enabled me to get to the finish line and it felt good. I distinctively remember saying, "Jesus, before you left this earth You fulfilled everything the Father asked of You, and before taking Your last breath, You said, "It is finished. Give me a finishing spirit."

I am currently in a position where I feel like I have mastered everything I can at this point, but at times I still feel unfulfilled. At work, I have been told I am an asset, and they are glad that I am on their team, but at times I do not see it in their actions. I do not see it in the responsibilities I am given, nor do I see it in a salary increase. I feel like I am just merely existing and counting down from the time I start working to the time I earn my paycheck. Days, weeks, months, and years go by and it seems like I am sitting and dwindling. I do not feel enthused, inspired, or encouraged. As soon as I get a spark, it just burns out as fast as I got it. At times there is a yearning on the inside of me for acceptance, but sometimes I get to the point where I block life out.

It makes me feel like I am in a bubble at work. People who know me will say good morning and ask how I am doing. I respond politely while screaming inside, "Do you really see me?" Sometimes I'm just numb walking through the halls at my workplace, like a zombie; I get up to go eat and come back down and sit at my desk. Sometimes I feel like I need work only because it brings more financial stability, but the work that I'm doing versus the work that I believe I am called to do are two different things. They are two different points in life that I'm trying to connect to help me feel satisfied and fulfilled. This was my thought on August 29, 2018, when the idea of a book came to my mind and here we are today.

I am ready to be fulfilled in what I do, working on my self-worth, my self-value, and moving beyond hurt. I deserve to be happy and not feel enslaved or in bondage. Don't get me wrong, I do not want to come across ungrateful because having a job and financial stability is a good thing, but I believe being fulfilled while you are working is much more rewarding. If we are working in our calling, or in our passion, I don't believe it should seem laborious, like a job. So, in this chapter of my life and this book, I am at a place where fulfillment is my mission, I will no longer tell myself that I cannot afford to be happy because there is strength in my waiting.

Chapter 3

REAL WORK LIFE

I could not have written this book without talking about Deaconess Gary, a lady from my church who babysat my daughter before she was able to go into daycare. One reason in particular that I can't forget her is that when she found out that I was walking from my home several times to her home because I had no money for transportation, she would be very upset with me. She would often say, "I would just have come and gotten you if you'd told me that you had to walk so far so early in the morning." I remember responding once, "But that would have been too much money to pay." I assumed I would have to pay her since I know people don't normally do favors for free. I also did not want to be a burden to her I was already thankful she was willing to watch my child for a small fee. Every time I would say that, Deaconess Gary would say, "My name is not people." When she could, she would take me half way to at least one bus stop on my route home, but I never felt comfortable about it. So, I stopped telling her when I did not have money to take the bus. I would just run in, pack up my child's bag, and run out the door, saying, "I'll see you later Deaconess Gary" before she could ask me anything. I was never raised to tell people my problems for sympathy or empathy.

We were bought up to problem solve and move on. During the times when I did not have enough money to catch the bus from Philly to Valley Forge, I would get up early in the morning and the Lord would tell me to prepare myself for work as if it was a normal day. I remember one time I only had money to catch one of the four buses needed to get to work; the bus started coming down the street, and I prepped myself to tell the driver that I did not have any money and see if he would allow me to ride. The bus rolled up at the stop, and the doors flung opened, as I looked up at the driver and I went to step up on the stairway, something told me to look down. As I looked down, there laying on the ground was a new crisp five-dollar bill. I picked it up so fast. I moved to put it in the farebox when the driver looked at me and said, "That's too much money." He began to ask people on the bus if anybody had change but nobody did, so the driver said, "Don't worry about paying." I did not understand then what God was doing, but He was setting me up for now.

Days gradually began to get better, because my income became steadier. I felt more comfortable sending my daughter to pre-K since she was getting older. I had to restructure how the babysitting would work out going forward; I wanted her in an academic childcare environment. So I enrolled her in daycare, which was similar to a school system where she would be getting the education and learning tools for a kindergartener since I was working all the time, sometimes multiple jobs. I transitioned her out from babysitting with Deaconess Gary to a childcare facility. This particular daycare included schooling and overnight care, and since I worked so late at nights, she could be in one location receiving the necessary schooling she needed for grade school. I remember one day, one of my friends jokingly said to me, "Oh the daycare is raising your child" and that really hurt me, because I was doing my best to provide for my child and provide a good environment for her education.

I was so annoyed, I said to her, "Don't you ever say that daycare is raising my child, because they are not raising my child, I am!" I would take the time with my child to take her to parks, Disney on Ice shows, and movies. We even attended award ceremonies together, celebrating her educational achievements. We would always find time to talk about her day, things that went on, or things she wanted to do the next time I took off work. I knew that there was not much I could do when it came to finances, because work was my only means of income. I had to make sure we had money to keep a roof over our heads and food on our table because there was a time when food was very low, and we did not eat in two days and I started regurgitating.

Working all the time started to take a toll on my child because I was not around, and she began to act out in school. The school could not understand her actions because she was so smart academically; she always got awards and outstanding achievements. The issue was that she just wanted to have me around more, but I had to work. I did not know then how much my not being around was impacting her. My daughter really couldn't understand either. She would just see me crying sometimes and see me struggling. I still had an undeveloped mentality dealing with important issues. I just did not know how to fix things other than working, but it had taken a toll on me too. You could tell my daughter wanted to help but all she would say is, "Mom, don't cry, I will try to be a big girl, and not get into trouble, I will do what I can to help you mom." I would try to explain to her how I had to work and how much I loved her. She loved me so much, but I knew she did not understand everything to the fullest. When she would speak so lovingly, it would just make me love her even more, I would hug and kiss her and reaffirm to her that we would make it. I will never forget those moments because I made a vow to never live like that again, and I never did.

I did not know then that I was prophesying my future. All I knew was that we were not ever going to go back to days like those again, where we could not eat, or when I had to spend so much time away from home to provide for my child. When I started working at Einstein main campus, I would use my badge to pay for food in the cafeteria when we needed food, and I counted this a blessing, but money was being deducted out of my pay for it and this impacted the money I needed for bills. So this became a problem financially again. I remember a colleague at work who would constantly provoke me and try to get me to react or respond in a way that would lead to a confrontation. I did my absolute best to ignore her and not let her insults get to me, not because I did not know how to handle myself, oh, I did! But I knew this was just a setup by the enemy to make me lose focus of the end goal. I knew why I was there and what the job meant to me. I needed to provide food, shelter, and other necessities for my child and myself, and I was not going to let the enemy win. News of our disagreements got to management and we were called into the office for a meeting with HR and other department heads to discuss what was going on between us. I knew going into the meeting that I was already at a disadvantage because she was friends with the director, and she got all the sympathy from the group, which was very disappointing. The conclusion from that meeting was that we should stay away from each other and avoid each other as much as possible so as not to have any further confrontations.

However, our paths crossed on one occasion after that meeting and there was no way to avoid it. So there again, she started to taunt me and at that moment I told myself, "No more, enough is enough!" I turned and said to her, "I am sick and tired of you bothering me, and if you dare put your hands on me, I am going to whoop you, right here in this hallway." Unbeknownst to me, while I was saying that to her one of the directors, who happened to be her good friend, was walking in the hallway and because my back was turned toward her, I didn't see her. My coworker, on the other hand, was facing that direction, so she saw her, and of course, she kept on insulting me so that I would keep talking, and when I turned around in that moment, I saw the director and was immediately gripped with fear. I thought I was going to be fired for sure because of this. It was not a moment I was proud of, but I had just reached my breaking point and I could not take the insults from her anymore.

So, after that unfortunate incident in the hallway, we got called in for another meeting. This time Lou from the HR department was brought in. When you saw Lou, you knew someone was getting let go, and I knew for sure, I thought for sure this time it would be me. I was definitely going to get fired. I kept thinking about the confrontation and how I handled it; I was not proud of it, but there is just so much a person can take. She had caused me a lot of emotional and psychological anguish, and I just could not take it anymore. I was sitting in my cubicle extremely nervous and waiting to hear what they had to tell me. When I walked into the room, everybody was smiling and I was even more nervous. They brought the incident up and the director narrated what she witnessed, and I just kept saying in my mind, "I am so fired!" But to my surprise, I was not! I could not believe it! I was told that if she and I got into another incident that I would be suspended and then they'd take subsequent actions if the situation necessitated it. I received a stern warning about a repeat incident and the results, which would be grounds for immediate termination. They then presented me with a document to sign agreeing to these conditions; I signed it in agreement.

I remember immediately feeling a roller coaster of emotions all at once after signing the agreement. When leaving the room, I turned to look everyone in the face only to see a lot of gloating, as if they just finagled me into a no-win situation by signing the papers. Time went on and there was still no change with the other person's actions toward me; after all that, she really did not ease off on her efforts to aggravate me.

The work environment became quite hostile and exceedingly hard for me to work effectively in, but I endured and kept doing what I was supposed to do. I recall her confronting me about something and I did not react, respond, or report the issue. But apparently, someone had witnessed the confrontation and reported it to HR, and before I knew what was going on, the director who was her friend was fired. Before she left, she came over to my desk. I did not expect her to come over to me or say anything to me because I knew she didn't like me, and the coworker that I was having conflicts with was her friend. I was incredibly surprised when she walked up to me and said, "Give me a hug. I just want to say good luck to you, kiddo! I wish you the best."

Immediately, I thought of the story of the three Hebrew boys who would not bow down and worship the king. The king ordered the mightiest men to turn the furnace up seven times hotter than it had been and then ordered them to throw the three boys into the middle of the fire that burned the hottest. This was where I felt I was, and just like the king's surprise when he looked back into the furnace and saw the four men, loosed, unharmed, and walking in the fire. The fourth man was the Son of God, who not only freed the boys in the fire, but made them able to walk around in the hottest part of the fire unharmed.

So when I was approached, I was dumbfounded and simply did not know what to say; all I could do was muster up the courage to say, "Okay, I wish you the best too." I still could not believe what had just happened. I didn't understand what God was doing but I knew He was with me, but to experience such an intense hostile situation and to come out unharmed was a testament to God's Word "no weapon formed against me will prosper." I was living that very portion of scripture. Yes, the weapon was formed, but it surely did not prosper, and I continued to experience God's immense favor after this. After the director left, her friend resigned, and I remained at that location for nine years. Then I applied and interviewed for another position at a different location in the network, and to my surprise another coworker at my current location interviewed for the same position.

They offered her the job, but I later found out that she wanted more money than they were willing to pay, so the hiring manager reached out to a manager that knew me and asked her to speak to me about possibly taking the job. I was told that the job would be a good fit for me and was informed about the pay they were willing to give me. I was able to negotiate my pay that still included the company raise that was scheduled to hit in a few months after being hired and an increase of my PTO time.

Although I was not the preferred candidate at first, God allowed me to become the most favored one. I must admit I was a little nervous about changing location since I had been at my current location for nine years, but I had confidence in doing the job I was hired for: I knew I had the ability to perform it well. So I started working in my new position and was given the authority to set things up as I needed to overturn the high reimbursement denial rate, as well as to improve reimbursements. The director was astonished by how methodically I worked and how quickly I was able to improve revenue. She saw how impeccable my work ethic was. When many workers in the department heard of this, they were not pleased because they thought they were not given the same praise for what they had contributed, so they attempted to hinder the progress. When the director gave me the authority to reorganize the department and supported me in every way I needed, this furthered the annoyance of many people. But now that I was a leader, I had to stay focused.

I always wanted to be a certain type of leader, and I wanted to develop into that, based on my experience in this new position. I wanted to be an authoritative and feared leader because this was the leadership style I was familiar with, it was what I saw throughout my work life. I thought I needed to embody that in order to lead in the workforce, demonstrating my power, being intimidating, threatening, and overpowering to get people to listen and do what I said, but I'm so glad I later learned that it is always better to be authentically me.

The leadership at the NovaCare billing office started to become very controlling, and I started seeing a different type of atmosphere. At that point I began filling out applications for other jobs, hoping they would come through, and I also pursued temp agency jobs as a backup. Things had gotten so bad that I took a leap of faith and accepted a temp job with the Ameri-Choice insurance company at the same location.

They found out about it over at NovaCare and were trying to block me from getting the job, but they were unsuccessful. The hiring manager at Ameri-Choice became more fascinated with hiring me because of the lengths taken to block me. So, even in this new position, I faced quite a bit of opposition from my coworkers, to the point where one physically hit me with a cabinet drawer on my back. One day I was in my cubicle area and this particular coworker was being very rude, and other staff were around who witnessed as she kept verbally confronting me. She then took the cabinet drawer and slammed it against my back. A coworker who was down the aisle heard what was going on and ran down to my area and stood in between us and said to the coworker that assaulted me, "You need to leave this area now!" This was very disturbing to see my coworkers standing around witnessing this assault and saying nothing, instead, they thought it was funny. Even one of the doctors who was there thought that it was hilarious. I just saw this as another level of test and trial that I was going through. I knew that God was with me the whole time because I did not respond physically. But I stood face to face with her and told her to move out of my cubicle before my other coworker had gotten up to intervene. I can say that the hand of God and His power has constantly been on my life, and every challenging test and trial drew me closer to Him and further away from me.

The issue was taken to HR and their resolution was to send both of us to a class to teach us how to get along. I could not believe it; I was physically assaulted and the way they chose to deal with it was to send us to a class? We both took the class together and were given a certificate of completion, to then "proudly" display at our workstation. A week later, she turned in her resignation letter after working in the company for over 30 years. Soon after she left, the department manager was fired and escorted off the premises by HR, and Lou who was now the head of HR was arrested, resulting from a sex trafficking and drug sting operation that was aired on TV. To see these things happening so rapidly around me was astonishing. After they left, I was plunged into more leadership roles and was able to obtain more skills as a result. But I was never given the official title in the department, only the responsibilities. The department began to evolve and was doing very well. More doctors were being hired, we began to see more patients in the office, and started doing over a thousand procedures monthly. Through it all I was still determined to wait on God. I was not legally aware of things like I am now, but I was not going to let anyone run me away from anything. If I was going to leave, it would be my choosing and nothing else, I had just as much right to work there as everyone else.

Looking back at it all now, I'm able to see that God was transforming the way I fight to His way of fighting, by waiting on Him to change things. This was when I began to triumph. Isaiah 40:31 says, "But those who wait on the Lord shall renew their strength. They shall mount up with wings like eagles, they shall run and not be weary, they shall walk and not faint." I may not have known about corporate legality, but God was my defense. I may have been laughed at and mocked, but God was my friend, protector, and provider. Yes, I felt the physical, emotional, and mental discomfort and disheartening of an unimaginable experience, but God was with me.

It was a different dynamic for us after the manager's departure. The staff started getting out of control and took advantage of the situation because the director rarely interacted with them, and by her being located on a different floor it allowed them to manipulate the issue even more. The administrative office and the actual physicians' office, where they saw patients, were on different floors. Prior to transitioning, the chair took over, and he hired different managers, but they never worked out. However, there were two managers that I would like to mention: The first one I had an exceptionally good working relationship with; we were quite close. She was certified in coding and knowledgeable in the field; she taught me a lot. Even though I had learned coding at Temple University, I never got my certification in it. So, to be able to learn all I was learning from her was amazing. Unfortunately, she began to change when things in the department didn't seem to go her way. You could tell that she was going through a lot at the time in her personal life. She had recently separated from her husband due to marital problems, and she was not taking care of herself; sadly, it affected her professional life as well. She entered into a relationship with a coworker's son who was also a patient, and of course, people started to whisper about it. Being that we had quite a good working relationship, I decided to approach her about the situation, and she became very angry at me, I guess, for having the audacity to speak to her about the issue. But I had approached her from a place of love, especially since her reputation as a manager was on the line.

Sadly, after that, she completely switched on me and tried all that she could to frustrate me in the department to get me fired. I could feel the aggression from every side, but I tried to focus on my work and not pay any attention to all the tactics that were used to frustrate me or cause me to slip up. She made sure that my overtime was taken away. Also, sometimes the vendors would come in and treat all the staff to lunch, but I was cut from that treat, and shown other petty behaviors. But I did not let that deter me from doing my job, performing all my duties and responsibilities the way I was supposed to.

I just kept encouraging myself that I would get through it.

She kept trying all she could to get me fired. She would present false stories to the chair of the department and I was constantly being called into meetings to get questioned about things that she said I did. At this point I knew that I would for sure be fired soon; I even started slowly taking my personal belongings that I had home. I did not want to be in a situation where, if I got fired, I would not be allowed to take anything with me, because this is what happened to the manager who was fired and escorted off the premises. She was not allowed to take any of her things on the day of her departure; she had to schedule a day and time when the office was closed to be escorted back on to the premises to get her personal belongings.

Killing my Goliath with kindness

Before transitioning into my academic career, my former director had resigned, but her assistant remained on the job. It was now the assistant's time to leave. She resigned and we had thrown her a party. My former director decided to attend the party and when she walked past the cubicle where I sat, she looked at me and said, "Oh Bev, you're still here in the same spot" and kept walking. I paused for a moment to process what she said. I told myself, now I can stand up and respond to her or I can hold my response. Well, I was not going to allow her to get to me by what she said, and the condescending message she was trying to send and that I was not going anywhere because she left and I was still in the same spot. She had no clue; I had no clue that I would see her ever again. So I just told myself, the devil is a liar. I was not going to feed into that, but it left a mark on me, it stuck with me for days, but God gave me the strength to keep on going. Well, unbeknownst to me, she had returned to Einstein for work because things did not work out so well for her after she left. I had emailed her to let her know the amazing things that I accomplished since her departure. I had graduated college, earned a leadership role in my area, and started my business. I forwarded my business (boutique) website address to her so that she could shop. (You will read more about these accomplishments and how they unfolded in chapters 4 and 5). I ended the message by saying, "I'm glad to hear you're back."

One Saturday morning, while I was at a church function, the manager called me; I was inclined not to answer in that moment and return her call after church, but she kept on calling, so I answered. When I did, she informed me that the chair physician had a heart attack – this was the one who was getting ready to fire me. I was shocked by the news, but told her I would pray for him and his family. I could not believe it, I knew without a doubt that I was going to be fired on Monday by this man, and here he had a heart attack before Monday. He was out for a good while recuperating from the heart attack, and I was back at work, doing everything that was expected of me. When he finally returned to the office, he was not pleased with how the manager was operating in the department and was about to fire the manager, but fortunately for her, she was transferred into another position, although it was a demotion from management. She stayed for a year or two in that position before retiring.

The chair physician hired a new manager; I knew of her in passing. I later found out her wife also worked in another department within the network. Prior to her being made manager in our department, she had served as one in a different department, where I seldomly interacted with her. We would politely exchange greetings but nothing more, so I did not know anything about her, I did not know she was married, who she was married to, or that her wife worked in the network. Now that she was the manager in my department, we were required to work closely, and of course, we bumped heads. She came in with an attitude of superiority and was very rude and bossy. Yes, I could have easily disregarded her rude and authoritarian demeanor, but she lacked the full understanding of how things were done in my area, and this kept us at odds. I took pride in my work. I was able to help align the office (front end) to flow with the standards of the billing office (back end) expectations, resulting in improved reimbursements and more revenue. But there she goes, trying to dismantle it all by replacing it with the way she ran her previous area. But this could not work both logically and sensibly because of the differences in specialties. That's why the friction was heavy.

The conflict between us kept brewing more and more because her way of managing and how she communicated her requests to me was not making much sense at all, especially since my experience was developed in the billing office (back end), which equipped me on how the front end should be aligned, which was the main reason why I was hired for the job. One day a colleague of mine, who witnessed the constant friction between us, pulled me to the side and explained she believed the real reason for the friction could be related to her sexual orientation, which may be fueling her desire to dominate me. Her sexual orientation was never an issue for me; I did not judge her on this or treat her differently because of it either. But it was noticeably clear that she was trying to instill some level of fear in me because she was the person in charge. There were others who also saw this; that my manager wanted me to be submissive to her, but that was not my personality. I wasn't a soft-spoken or timid person. I was always taught to exude strength and power, even as a child, and so I had an extraordinarily strong personality and I believe that is why we disagreed so much. She did all she could in order to get me fired, but thankfully, it did not work; she, on the other hand, ended up getting fired. During this time, the department chair was also working as the interim chair for the

Division of Medicine, and when he was not offered the job as the chair of the Division of Medicine he resigned as chair of the Department of Gastroenterology.

After his departure, the department merged with another division, and this division operated completely differently from what we were used to. The daily operations and the environment itself became extremely challenging because we merged with a division outside of the Division of Medicine. The managers were so much younger than us and very demeaning and disrespectful toward us. Many of those who came from my department left, as they did not want to deal with the frustration anymore; it was just too much. It was so discouraging and challenging, to the point where I was also ready to quit and walk away from the job that I had been at for the past 19 years

Sometimes you have to just take it!

There were many times that I wanted to leave; I wanted to just walk away like I had done as a teenager. I was not dealing with it well, but I couldn't do like I did then, because I had a child, I had somebody I was responsible for – someone to take care of and to feed. I could not just walk away. I had to take it, though it was painful, disturbing, and even embarrassing at times, I had to keep performing. I built up a wall to block out what was really going on and then tapped into the side of me that was numb to these things. I saw all that was going on, I felt the negativity, racism, and hate, but I just kept walking and carrying on as if nothing of the sort was happening. The issue is, I became so good at it and left it unchecked until it was time to deal with these emotions later in life. Yes, suppression is real, but when these things are not handled, they will resurface later, at the worst time in life.

I remember calling one of my older sisters one day to tell her I was ready to quit on that day. She knew I was really hurting, so she said, "Bev, can I just pray for you? You have a good job, things are very well in your life despite this, and God is blessing you. Let me pray for you." My sister's prayer calmed me down; I got renewed strength to keep going, taking it day by day.

As the department began to expand, I was placed in a different location that was more conducive for me to work effectively. My new director and chair were very supportive of me and made sure that I had everything I needed to balance my work and school schedules. The leadership style of the new chair and director was a mix of kindness, thoughtfulness, consideration, and support. They showed us respect as individuals and not just as workers, and this helped things to drastically change for the good, for so many of us. They were very inclusive and not authoritarian; they took time to get to know us and asked how we felt about things that impacted our working environment or daily operations. They were understanding of common things that impacted our families and home life, as well as things that constantly affected our jobs.

In the transition process from our previous department to this new one, management started to realize that a lot of the people who were working did not have the proper credentials or certifications, which was a liability for the network. So, they asked me to train them – I had the exceptional duty to train the second- and third-level leadership, directors, and managers on the various aspects of the GI department. Workers in the new area were astounded and kept wondering who I was that top leadership were coming into my cubicle to get trained.

My director was the first leader I encountered throughout my career who showed respect to every worker and didn't see herself as high and mighty. She was kind, patient, and didn't mind saying, "I'm sorry." The way she dealt with us and interacted with the staff was unmatched. She showed genuine concern for the well-being of every staff person. I wasn't used to this kind of leadership, and I just kept questioning if it was real because of my previous experiences. I was just waiting for something to go wrong but she was different, she was an amazing leader; and this was the kind of leader I wanted to be.

Cut short by chaos

As I began to build up time and started my transitioning process into another position, I began to be more involved in different areas. We had a meeting with a team of leaders in a round table discussion about billing and claim issues, revenue, and how to better bridge an understanding of billing from the front end to align to what we do on the back end in the billing department. I was very knowledgeable about how things could improve, and because I was familiar with understanding the insurance aspect of billing and the provider and facility aspect of billing, I was able to bring a clear understanding to the discussion. As I was speaking, suddenly someone came to the door and I will never forget the fear on her face when the door flew open, and she said, "Everyone needs to leave now and go get your kids."

We all stopped and looked at her in silence because we did not know what was going on. She said, "Airplanes have just hit the World Trade Center in New York, we are under attack, go home now." This was how I found out about the dreadful attacks of 9/11. It was unbelievable and frightening to hear, so we all rushed back to our desks, collected our belongings, and left. And all you would hear about on every media platform and channel was about the planes striking the Twin Towers. I ran in panic along with everybody in the department, to go get to my child. When I got to her and grabbed her, she started asking me what was going on. I was shaking in so much fear and shock, I couldn't answer her.

I didn't know if the attacks were heading to Philly. The world appeared to be in chaos and Philadelphia was in chaos too. There was mad traffic and confusion. At that point, all I could think about was how good it felt to hold my child and to get home. When we got home, I told her what was going on because no one had watched TV or listened to the radio in school; they were all teaching and going about their normal routine. I put the TV on, and we just sat and watched the news together. This was the turning point in America; things would change forever. It changed things professionally and personally in people's lives. There were so many different things going on at the same time. However, this occurrence shook things up; people started to be much nicer to each other at the job. People began to show they cared; they even started to embrace one another.

Chapter 4

MY BC YEARS – BACK TO THE BEGINNING

So, everyone has a BC (before Christ) stage in their life. During my BC years, I started drinking Olde English 800 malt liquor during my mid-teenage years. I never knew about wine or any fancy drinks growing up in the 'hood. I, along with the guys I hung out with, liked the 40-ounce bottles. As I mentioned, girls and I did not get along; there was just too much bickering and cattiness. When I would hang with the guys, they were more authentic; they would tell you how they felt and not hide behind any games. So I felt myself gravitating to the guys on the corners versus hanging with the girls. I would drink and get high. I would get high from smoking weed wrapped in the blunts that I was introduced to.

One of my siblings that I was close with would also smoke with me, and after smoking we would be so hungry when we got home. We had the munchies and were always looking for something to eat. It was then that my mother's style of parenting changed. She stopped hitting us or speaking in threatening tones. I think she started to seek God more on how to get through to us in a different way. I remember she would say to us, "Y'all keep huffing and puffing. You're going to blow your house down" referring to us smoking.

I believe I was doing all that I was doing to get attention; I just wanted to impress others. One day I drank so much I threw up all over my mom's bathroom floor, then stumbled to my bed and passed out. I remember waking up to my mom's voice asking, "Where did this mess come from, who did, this? When I find out who did it, I'm putting them out today." I could not even get myself together, I was that drunk. When she came to my room and smelled it on me, she said, "Beverly, did you do this?" With the smell of liquor on me, throw-up residue, and me standing half straight, I responded, "No, mom, I didn't do that."

My mom stood there and looked at me; she stood and stared at me shaking. I started thinking to myself, "Oh my God, she is going to kill me." But instead, she just said, "Okay, close the door" and went in and cleaned up the bathroom. I did not hear anything else from her after that. This is one of the main things I was referring to in other chapters when I said I did not want this life for my daughter. I did not want that to pass down to her because I was aimlessly living during my teenage years without knowing I was. The only motivation I had was by watching TV and instantly thinking that one day I would become a judge. Whenever I was asked what I wanted to be at school or church, I would always say, a judge. Unfortunately, that would not be the case because the resources to pursue that career were not available to me. What was available to me was going to the corner, hanging out with the dudes, and connecting with the wrong people, getting into trouble. That was all I looked forward to. Soon after that, I started wanting fast money, and the guys on the corner, started showing me how to make fast money by selling drugs.

Then, it turned into, take what you want: If you want a car, go ahead, and take it. If you want to go here or there, just go; if you want to ride in it, you can afford to. Just go take it from the stores. It sounded intriguing, but I was always nervous to steal from the stores. I didn't know why, and when I saw my friends doing it, I would get upset. I could not do it, I was scared. Then my friends started popping pills. At the time it was ecstasy pills that were all the rage in the market. I wanted no parts of it; I continued to do marijuana. I saw the effect it had on them, how it turned them into totally different people. They were like zombies and I was not okay with that. I was okay with smoking blunts and drinking the Olde English.

One day a friend of the group tried to have a mutual friend take a whole pill, but she refused, so the friend told her she'd split the pill with her. She split the pill. However, my friend did not take her portion of the pill, but the other girl did. She took the pill and she died. We were all high school students at the same school. I was sad when she died, but I was also grateful that my friend did not take that pill because she would have died too. That scenario was a wake-up call because remember, my mother did not even know I was being exposed to all of this stuff. I was not raised like this; although I was raised in a neighborhood that was involved in this kind of lifestyle, I was brought up to shun it. But instead I gravitated to it even though my mother was strict.

She was the kind of mother that had locks on the doors and windows to prevent us from going out because she did not want us to hang out with certain people she deemed were "of the world." She did not want that. So, when she saw us starting to build relationships with these people, she would tell them, okay, if you want to be my daughter's friend, you all will have to come to church because that is what we do. Needless to say, as kids, that did not go over well. I had siblings who would test the waters and when mom would lock the door, they would go out the window. They would say, "Oh, that's mommy talking that church stuff again, about the fear of the Lord and threatening us about going to hell." If we were supposed to eat certain food and ate chocolate instead, we were going to go to hell because we disobeyed God's dietary law. We could not straddle the fence in her house: We were either going to be a saint and stay or a sinner and go.

I did not want to go to hell, so I decided to classify myself as a sinner who needed God's mercy. Fear was the apparatus used for us to identify with God. I don't think it was used in a way to represent God in a negative way though. I think it was used in a way to get us to reverence God, to acknowledge God, and to understand that He doesn't tolerate sin.

The scripture in Proverbs 22:6 says, "Train up a child in the way they should go so when they are old, they won't depart from it." I felt a lot of my behaviors in those days were being influenced by the world. I was dealing with a lot and I was just trying to compartmentalize my thoughts the best way I could.

But I knew God knew my heart. Though I didn't know Him the way I needed to know Him, He knew me. I knew enough of Him to get it right. I knew right from wrong and was convicted to make it right.

Though my mother primarily used fear, it was good for me, because the enemy wanted to deceive me. That is why we have to be careful of how we get the Word across to our children and to our youth, to let them know that they are created in God's image, which makes them representatives of God. When we take that Word of God and present it in a fashion that displays God's nature, it makes it plain to them, but when we don't, they will question God and form doubts in their minds. We have to be careful as parents when we do that; those were the things that impacted me and my parenting skills with my daughter the most. I am more accountable now when I reflect on what I went through as an adolescent and how my mother tried to get the fear of God in me. And that fear was to get me to revere God, but it pushed me away. So I knew in raising my daughter, that I wanted to tweak that part of parenting to bring about more reverence and less fear.

Chapter 5

MY DAUGHTER HELPED ME TO FIND ME

After coming into this new enlightened awakening, I had to ask God to show me how to raise my daughter, because I did not know how to do that. I wanted to raise her in the admonition of the Lord and keep her away from the negative things I was pulled into. My mother did all she could to raise me well, though I strayed, but it was definitely not her fault. And this is why I said before that I wasn't ready to be a responsible adult. I was not ready for the world in this aspect, but having my child and working and going through the various things I went through matured me and made me ready.

One is supposed to learn during different stages of life, but by becoming pregnant and having a child so early, it forced things to start happening sooner, faster, and more aggressively so that I could start learning, and get a good understanding of who I needed to become. I am proud of having my baby because if it was not for her, I may have not lived to see the goodness of the Lord, with all the unfruitful friendships I had leading me down the wrong path. I was pushing my own self to the backseat. After getting the help to go back to school and to start working, I decided to cultivate what God had cultivated in me. I knew it would have influenced me differently.

I turned the negative into positive; I decided to cultivate my daughter too. I would ask her, "What do you want to be baby?" And I started to find programs and resources to put her into that would mold her into a rounded person, from cheerleading to volleyball to SAT testing programs. I wanted her to be able to take the test and pass at a level acceptable for college and not just any college, but a prestigious one. And she did just that. I remember one summer when she had to live on Temple University campus because her program required her to in order for her to remain in the program. It was hard for both of us.

There were a lot of sacrifices; she had to give up things as a teenager. But one thing I told her was that I wanted her to have a childhood, because I felt like my childhood was taken away from me because I had to always watch people's children. I had to watch my sibling's children when I came home from school. One of my oldest siblings who I did this for would be out with my mother because my mom would cook pies and make dinners to help the fundraising projects for the church. We attended a small church, and we needed funds to fix the building and pay the bills. So my siblings would go out and sell pies with mom; staying home with the babies was my duty. Sometimes when they finished doing church duties, they would go out shopping for church clothes and adornments, at times from morning and they wouldn't be back home till night, and there I was just watching the children. That took a toll on me and I decided that I did not want to have a lot of kids. I felt like that robbed me of my childhood. That broke me and created its own emotional fracture. This did not affect my love for my nieces and nephews though.

My mother taught my older sisters how to run the house and take care of the younger children, and when an older sibling would leave home, the next one would graduate into the mom role to help out, because my mother had to do so much on her own to keep the family together. This meant all I had to look forward to was school, church, and babysitting. I did not want that for my daughter. And when my daughter became a teenager, and she wanted to make money and came to me about babysitting, I was defiant. "You will not babysit anybody's babies," I told her. She could not understand why I was so passionate about it. She would say, "But mom, this is the only way people my age make money." But I vehemently said no. I told her that she was going to have to find a job. So, when she was around 13 or 14 years old she started job hunting, and for two years my daughter went filling out applications for jobs. And the place that took her application was a restaurant called Qdoba. Though they hired her almost immediately, she had to wait until she was 16 years old to start working. It couldn't be official until she was the legal age to work.

We were so excited for her to start working there. I felt so proud of her; she was a teenager who could be doing teenage things but instead she chose to work. I didn't want to strip away from her the need to make money, but I knew babysitting was not it because of how it affected me. I always found myself comparing my decisions as a child to the current issues for my child. I did not want her to be negatively affected by the things that affected me growing up. So, I would always ask her how did this or that make her feel? I wanted to demonstrate care to her in a way that was not demonstrated to me. I would sit down with her and come up with options and solutions to things and create a game plan. For example, I had asked her, "Outside of babysitting, where do you see yourself working?" And that's when she said, "Oh, I could work at a fast-food restaurant."

I allowed her to tell me what she wanted to do and not me telling her what to do. That was my way of strategizing, where she got a say, where she got to be heard. I was still learning; I wanted to be a good mom for her. Not a mom who stripped her of her feelings or ideas. At this point, everything was about my child because I had lost the aspiration to cater to myself. I started to live my life implicitly through her and her needs like most parents do.

In this segment, I will backtrack a little to things mentioned in earlier chapters. I had repeatedly got lost in the cycle of living for my daughter. I was doing everything for her, every breath, every move was for her. When I started thinking about school, I thought, okay, how am I going to help her with school because I do not have the finances for both of us to have a degree. So I started inquiring about financial aid while attending CCP, where I had started taking night classes at Einstein. During that time, Einstein was having big layoffs back to back, and it was my desire to obtain at least two degrees before being terminated, so I prayed to God to allow me to stay in order to obtain this goal. Prior to this time, I had not been to school in 20 years. And since I had worked at Einstein for so long, and gave so much of myself during my twenties, had gone through so much there as you've read previously, I felt like they owed me more than just a regular paycheck.

I figured if not, and if I got laid off, my pension would be little to nothing. Fortunately, I started going to CCP on Einstein's campus. I hoped that my daughter would help me with tutoring because she had already gone through similar material while prepping for acceptance to college. Though I was scared, I was happy to have a young daughter who was currently in school and doing relatively well to help me. Her grades were consistently high, so they put her in a special class like they did me years ago in high school.

I remember when they scheduled me to take a placement test at the college. For some reason when the date came, I was flooded with much fear and doubt. I was asking myself, how I am going to go take this test with a bunch of kids who are coming out of high school, and I don't know if I can. I felt inferior and I felt like I did not want to do it. On the day, it began to rain and I kept talking myself out of it, but the more I kept saying, "You know that giving up and excuses are not an option." When I looked up, it was 15 or 20 minutes to the time that I was supposed to be at the location to take the placement test and I hadn't even left my home yet. The location was at least 35 to 40 minutes away. But all I heard in my spirit was, "Just go to school, take the test, just go take it." Still, as I was getting dressed, I was talking myself out of it.

I got in my car, still talking myself out of doing this and as I was driving down the street, the rain kept pouring. Then as I started to get closer, I changed the story I kept telling myself to "You know what, they probably just got finished because it's past the time so I might as well just turn around." Nevertheless, I kept on going until I got there. I parked my car and started walking toward the door. I got to the front desk where the security was, and realized that I didn't even have the ID to get in. To me, that was confirmation to turn around and go home. Until the security guy said to me, "Just give me your name; I can pull you up from the records in the system and give you a temporary card."

After looking me up in the system he said, "Okay, the placement test you're scheduled for is running late. If you look around the corner you will see a long line; everybody is waiting to get in there, so just go around the corner." I went around the corner and there it was, a long line and the people who were supposed to give the test hadn't even arrived yet. I went and sat down, but I was so fearful. I was seeing so many young people, and despite seeing a few mature people too, I still felt like running out of there. I was just beating myself down. I did that, not knowing that I was feeding into the enemy's plan.

Ten minutes went by and I got up to when there came the people who were running the session for the test. They came in soaking wet, saying "We're here." I had no choice but to go in and take the electronic test. The questions were not as bad as I thought they'd be, yet I continued to beat myself up about the possibility of doing badly. I was glad when it was over. When my name was called to receive my scores, I was told that I placed at a remarkably high level. The grade I received was above most of the high school graduates. I was shocked. I was totally amazed. I felt like they were lying to me or playing with me because it made no sense. The lady reporting the results said, "Ms. Davis, I'm telling you the truth." I continued to doubt myself even when the proof was showing contrary to what I thought; it was so sad how I did not even think I was good enough to pass a college placement test. I started my first college course in December 2013 at CCP on Einstein's campus. Some processes, principles, and basic concepts were challenging to grasp since I hadn't been in school for years. I figured, well, I have a high schooler at home so she can help me. But to my surprise, my daughter would tell me at times, "I can't do this with you mom. It's too much; you don't want to listen, and you question everything. You need to get a tutor." I thought that was the worst thing she could have ever said to me. I would do anything and was doing everything for her. She said, "Mom, you are too difficult to help; just go to the school for help. They have resources that can help you. They provide paid tutors." I felt so embarrassed, but I went back to the main campus and got a tutor and those tutors gave me the time, patience, and training I needed to succeed. I thought because I was working in professional settings that I was doing things professionally; however, I came to find out that I did not know how to write academically.

At school they began to help me with structuring my writing properly and with my oral communication. That's when I started to understand what my daughter meant when she said it was difficult to help me because I needed to understand some basic concepts. And I was not allowing her to show me these concepts without asking questions, but that's me: When I'm curious or learning something new, I tend to overthink things. I started to learn things that I remembered learning in high school. I started with algebra, then moved to English, and then research methodology, and that's how I started to build my academic knowledge.

Yes, I was building momentum. The more I began to pass my courses, the more inspired I became. And I didn't pass them with low grades. I passed them with A's and B's, so the more A's and B's I received, the more I would want. Though I wanted more A's than B's because when I got the B's, I did not feel right in my spirit. I wanted to be perfect in my studies. Achieving an A signified excellence to me, but to get a B after reaching a state of excellence was unacceptable. I didn't always want to be perfect because I felt I didn't deserve it; however, I began to realize, I am God's created perfection. The handiwork of His perfection. So, everything I do comes from the perfected excellence of God. Therefore, I could never look at myself as a perfectionist because God is the only perfectionist among men, so when I didn't get an A, it made me upset because I knew I could reach the place of excellence consistently if I continued to trust in God.

This way of thinking started to transfer to other areas of my life. I wanted to get each of my degrees separately: the associate's, the bachelor's, and then my master's. Studying for my degrees exposed me to different experiences, cultures, and people. I met people from diverse backgrounds and cultures, and I really enjoyed learning from them too. I was able to make friends with people who celebrated me. This was new to me: I had never experienced this before in my entire adult life, only sporadically during childhood, but that was it. Although I was developing culturally, I still had a "hood" approach and a church mentality to some things. Crazy, huh? Now that I look back on it, I don't know how in the world God was able to do what He did with me, but I see now that it took the necessary pain to transition me into purpose.

The Bible tells us how to treat people who are different from us. I started to understand this more. I came from a culture of strong leaders in the church. I see the church as more prominent in leadership but not as an affluence in the community, government, or in the school system. I wasn't accustomed to the type of leadership in the world: My mother was a vigorous leader who demonstrated entrepreneurship because she didn't want to work a regular nine-to-five job. My father worked different types of gigs, before starting his own businesses.

During the times when my father wasn't around, my mother worked as a baker. She was also good at making clothes. She went back to college while raising us. She'd never felt like a regular job was her thing, and let's not forget that she was raising twelve kids, by itself that was doing multiple jobs. Knowing how impactful all these things were on my life, I wanted to help others from similar backgrounds as mine to achieve more for their lives, too. I did not have an independent desire to read the Word of God on my own, other than for the purpose of going to Sunday Bible School, which again was a requirement enforced by my mom. The same thing goes for prayer. When it was time for family prayer, we prayed or I would pray if my mom was going to deal with an issue with a person in the church. I had to do this when my mom went to pray for that someone just in case evil spirits decided to come back to the house. That was the only time I prayed, and again, this was out of fear. Suffice to say I did not have a relationship with Christ, just an awareness of God and His work. I did not understand the implication when it was constantly taught that I needed to get to know Christ on my own and in my own way. I only knew God by what my mom told me, what the church taught me, but I still did not understand precisely. In my young mind, all I could think was that I was going to miss out on something fun, exciting, and great.

I drew all my life's reference from the law laid down by my mother and the church. This made me have aggression and anger towards God: I had many questions for Him. It was then I started to understand when Jesus said, "I didn't come to do away with the law, but I come to fulfill it," Matthew 5:17. He wanted people to understand the law and the Word, and He knew that this could only be done by allowing the Word itself to take on flesh. This made us to see how practical the Word is. Christ did not do away with what my mother taught me; He came to make it clear, though some things were truly my mother's doing and not God's, but I still made it, so I'm not mad about it. I eventually found a yearning in me to want more, to do more, and to better myself not only academically and professionally, but biblically. Everything started happening simultaneously. I graduated from CCP in December 2016. That was the best feeling of my life, to face my childhood fear and make it disappear.

Before I graduated, I started putting things together to start working on my bachelor's degree at the University of Philadelphia, which later merged with Thomas Jefferson

University. I graduated from Thomas Jefferson University with a Bachelor of Science in health services management, in 2018. I started my graduate program with Temple University in 2019, a Master of Public Health (MPH) degree in health policy and management, and I'm scheduled to graduate in 2021. I remember taking an emergency prevention and preparedness course at Thomas Jefferson University taught by a professor who was a police sergeant. This inspired me to get a degree in public health, which would allow me to work in various areas of healthcare, including public health agencies, government, and law organizations.

Taking this course was so exciting for me: I examined footage of the 30th Street train wreck and Hurricane Katrina. I was inspired by how they were able to partner with other health agencies, and public health agencies to help people in need. That's what I wanted to do too. I like helping people, especially the elderly and the youth. Those are the most vulnerable people in our population during a crisis or normally in life and it just was so inspirational to see. This is how I got into the public health field.

I started putting it in the atmosphere by saying, "I want my master's and a PhD in public health," but I just didn't know the actual area that I wanted to start in." One day, the new chairman of the Division of Medicine, the division I once worked for, got a whiff of my goals, and set up a time for us to meet to go over some information that could help me succeed. Dr. Ford was well connected to John Hopkins University in Baltimore. In the meeting he said to me, "Listen, I want you to do your public health degree program at John Hopkins University. I know the Dean, and I know you. I want to help you with your entry letter." I was so astonished by his willingness to see me succeed, and on a big scale, but John Hopkins offered an MPH degree at 70% online and 30% through residential associating courses including a year of field work. I was not sure I could do that at all.

I knew that would be challenging because I still had a daughter that I had to attend to, and I still needed to work. So, I knew that it wasn't feasible for me. Then I considered Temple University's College of Public Health because they were willing to omit my GRE exams because I had a high GPA, a 4.0. They also waived the deposit fee.

So I went back to Dr. Ford and told him my plans. That's when he agreed to give me the letter of recommendation. I adopted him as my mentor: He always gave me great advice and took the time to accommodate me whenever I needed it. I was accepted into Temple's College of Public Health graduate program and I was ecstatic. Every relationship has its challenges; my relationship with my daughter is no different. She is now developing into young adulthood. She's no longer a teen, but a young adult heading to college. She finished high school and now she wants to do her thing. She doesn't see the world like her mom, she sees things differently, which causes a struggle between us at times. Just like any mother and daughter relationship, when your children are growing up it's hard for you to let go.

When my daughter told me she wanted to live on her own it brought tears to my eyes because I instantly interpreted it as the fact that she didn't want to be with me anymore. But this was not the case; she simply wanted to figure some things out for herself. I still felt so crushed when I heard this; it was like a dagger to my heart. It was very painful and hard for me to accept, but I couldn't expect anything less of her, since I had exemplified the same thing with trying to find my independence in life. This is what I've been showing this girl from day one. It's hard for me to grasp. It's hard for me to accept. I will never forget when we had that conversation.

Before she even went to college, I was in a state of mourning because ever since she was born, it has always been me and her. This was a real hard thing for me to deal with. I remember the week she moved to college, I just kept crying; I cried myself to sleep. I cried everywhere, walking down the street, crying at my workstation, I just cried and cried at the thought of being separated from my child, because she was my only family that has been consistently around, and now we were being separated. She became the friend I never had, someone I could go home and tell my problems to. Now all of this was ending. When my daughter was younger, I tried dating, but she was so distraught over it that I put that part of my life on hold to give her what she needed to be okay. I did not think twice, after seeing her cry and beg me not to allow someone to come into our life's that could possibly take me away from her. This little girl was highly intelligent and smart, she was always wise beyond her years, and was courageous to speak up.

I was so scared for my daughter going to college in another state because I thought people would take advantage of her. Even though I was scared, she was not. She has always been a brave child and she was ready to tackle it. When my mother and I took her to college, we drove; I remember getting home that night, and stopping in the middle of the street screaming and crying because it was like someone had passed away for me. Our separation was extremely hard for me to handle.

It was then that the spirit of God said to me, "Do it for you." I began to say I would go up to her school to help her. He said, "No, now do it for you." I heard Him audibly say it. So I continued driving and crying. I had no clue how to do "it" or do it for me, but God started guiding me and helping me.

I did not understand what it meant to be on my own. I was depressed, though I did not identify that it was depression at the time, but I was definitely depressed. I did not know that the separations and rejections I had experienced in my early years affected me until they resurfaced as I drove back. I guess it was the perfect time for it to resurface because I was taking courses in psychology and learning different things and understandings about mindsets, decisions, and emotions. I was able to diagnose myself and identify what I was going through. I was in a deep depressive state. I wouldn't eat, I couldn't cope, I was sick, and I would work for long periods at the job as a coping mechanism. Then I'd go home and stay up working on schoolwork. I would dress myself in my work clothes and become terribly busy. But when the depression hit, I would just eat and sit and watch TV. My health was going downhill rapidly after I'd been maintaining it for years.

After visiting the doctor I was told I was facing hypertension. I also was unable to get my blood pressure down for months. It was so high, I was heading for a stroke, and I couldn't stop it. I kept saying, "I don't know how to fix it." I didn't realize I was contributing to it because I wasn't sleeping. I did not realize that everything that I was doing, not sleeping, working late, and not exercising, had added to the problem so rapidly. But even though the depression was coming out in the ugliest ways, it was beneficial because it was teaching me how to handle the things I had suppressed early in life. God had to force these things to come this way because I wouldn't voluntarily do it because my mind wasn't structured that way. Family issues, work issues, single-parent issues, lack of support, lack of relaxation; Just work, work, work, work!

I lost sight of myself and it was challenging trying to figure things out, so much so that my daughter would often say to me, after the way I behaved, "That's not my mother at all." She would say, "Mom, you were always so strong, and you never let things get to you like this. What is going on?" but I could not get a handle on things. I have always thought the world of my daughter. She always achieved in school, then went on to attend Howard University, an HBCU, graduated, and then moved to California to start a new life with an amazing company. I was proud of my baby. All I wanted to see was her going to college. I was happy that she made it through high school without getting pregnant or having a baby by 20, I was happy about that. Because these were my fears since I had gotten pregnant and had a child at 20. Not only did she make it through high school without getting pregnant, she then went on and graduated from Howard University. This was huge!

I remember her saying, "You know, mom, it's sad to hear you talk so remorsefully about the things going on in your life. It's sad and I really want things to be better for you," she continued "I don't understand how you were able to give me so much love and so much support when you didn't even have it, and you didn't receive it consistently like how you had given it to me." That's because I had realized early on that I needed to give her what I had needed.

I longed to be shown love, but I suppressed my feelings regarding rejection and pulled what was left from my heart to give love to my child in the way I wanted for myself. But now all of these feelings and more started to resurface. They started to come back up when I felt rejected by her leaving for college, then moving to California. You know, I never knew by mirroring how well my mother pushed forward in times of struggles in her life, it would turn out to impact me so deeply. This part was missing; it was never shown to me so that I could model it. I was lost, I was hurting, I was uncertain about this new thing and I just could not understand what was going on. All I did was cry, eat, and watch TV to cope.

It started being very heavy on me emotionally, where I would just really feel like I was a nobody, I was not celebrated, was not told, "Oh, good job! This is good" or "That was done well." When I graduated it was like, "So what? Yeah, okay." This is how I judged what I did and who I was. My daughter encouraged me to go to a therapist and I told her I wasn't going to any therapy. "That's for crazy people and I am not crazy," I told her.

I ended up going and I'm glad I did. Therapy helped me to see that my voice matters. My therapist helped me to see that my bruises matter and I can have a difference of opinion and still be your equal and not inferior to anyone. She helped me to see some things about me like my strength, and she helped me to acknowledge my weakness. For me to only acknowledge my strengths and not my weakness was not good behavior. Even how I communicated about it to convince people, I was really trying to convince myself. She helped me to see that there is nothing wrong with me. She made me know I am a normal person. Because I thought I was abnormal. I thought something was wrong with me. I thought those things that I struggled with so long as a child, that made me angry and always, wanting to fight, were my fault.

The therapy sessions broke ground for God to start bringing up something new; whatever He had destined for me, it started coming out. He started to cultivate me even more and build me more. And it penetrated every aspect of my life. How I dealt with my daughter and our relationship started to change. I could not deal with it in anger anymore. I could not deal with it through just shutting down. I had to start dealing with it head on because the way I dealt with it before was to run away from it; I was avoiding it, not confronting it. I was now becoming mentally and emotionally stronger and learning how to deal with things again. I stopped fighting with my hands because of not being heard, and I now speak because of how powerful my voice is being heard. God knew how to use my daughter to help lead me to a place to find help to find myself, but I had to get up and go, and to apply what I now know.

I now had the tools to communicate. It was fine for me to feel different and to feel angry. Anger is a normal response, but how one reacts in that anger, how one takes that anger out is what makes the difference. I was growing. I was still going through the process of being me; I would at times still attach myself to past behavior until I decided this is not what I am going to continue to do. But because that pattern had been practiced so long, it took some time for me to let it go. I started to replace the acceptance of friends' negativity with things like "If we are friends, this is how I would like to be talked to." Or "No, please do not talk to me like that. Please do not treat me like that. You will not do me like that, or this relationship will be over unless it can become more effective." This mindset was transferred over to my job and to every other relationship.

Chapter 6

GOD'S CALLING ON MY LIFE

I started to lean on God in a new way, working on conquering my flesh; this was one of the areas in my life that I struggled with the most. Glory to God I started growing in His grace and in His Word, in prayer and growing up in fasting. As I slept one night, I had a dream of me preaching and it felt so real. In the dream, I was in the congregation, yet I was up preaching and in front of a lot of people, the Spirit of God was moving so strongly that I jumped out of my sleep wondering what was going on. I started saying, "Oh no, I'm not doing that." It shook me up, and I could not go back to sleep for hours. This was one I was going to keep to myself.

I kept talking to God about what He showed me, and I would remind Him, "God you know it's me, right? What are you doing? It is me. I cannot do stuff like this." Years went by and I kept it to myself and continued my life. Soon I was asked to be on the usher board at church. I was ushering, as I kept going to church, and I became more involved in the ministry, not just in church. My personal life was improving with God as my prayer life improved. I was sitting up from nighttime to morning studying, just thirsty for God's Word, I was eating it up, wanting more of it, and digesting it. My character started to change and those things that I did not want to acknowledge or realize I had to deal with, I started to process. A good number of years went by. It was around 2013 when I got another visitation, this time I heard in my spirit, "Go tell your pastor, I called you to preach."

Again, I was like, "I cannot do that." I would go to church, feel the Spirit, but just kept it going.

Sometimes I would be asked to lead prayer service, devotion, and complete some speeches. When they asked me to do speeches or to be involved, I could hear the Spirit say, "You can do it" but I would just keep on going, ignoring what I heard. I'll never forget when the Holy Spirit wanted me to go tell my pastor about me preaching. I kept saying, "I am not ready, and I cannot do that."

One day I decided to visit the old church where I recommitted my life to Christ; I visited with my daughter. I tried to go back for good but I could not because I felt like these people were too holy and I felt like I didn't fit in because I was not. I was not at that place in my life because I had other things going on. I looked at their external presentations and how they praised God and I thought there was no way possible I could be that holy.

In the middle of smoking a cigarette one day, after attempting to try church and feeling inadequate and complaining yet again to God about how imperfect I was and how perfect everybody in the church seemed to be. I repeatedly told God, "I cannot do it." I heard the voice of God say, "Do it or end up in hell." That's the way He said it. I was so shaken up, my cigarette dropped. I was shaking literally from the inside out, and I said, "God, if you teach me, I'll do it." He had had enough of me complaining and giving excuses because He knew what He could do in my life. And He has been teaching me ever since and taking me to another level to preach for Him.

On another occasion as I was heading about my business. I heard God say, "I want you to go to church tonight, and I want you to tell your pastor, that I have called you to preach." We had church on Wednesday and Friday nights and ,of course, on Sundays. This time I said, "God, I got it, I love You. I respect You. I honor You. Please give me some more time; I can't do it yet."

He told me that early in the morning. By noon when I was going about my day, I noticed the doors of the elevators at my job were having issues closing and they were moving slowly. It was moving weirdly but was not stopping, neither were the doors opening. So I got on to go about my daily routine. I got on the elevator, but then thought maybe I did not push the right button because when the doors closed the elevator moved but never stopped on the floor that I wanted. I began pushing buttons, then the elevator started to go faster but the doors were still not opening; none of the buttons could stop it. This was when God said, "I will put you through this floor." I said, "Oh Jesus, if You open the door, I'll go tell my pastor, and I'll go tell the world; just open the door, please. You don't have to break my legs, You don't have to kill me, just open the door." The doors flung open. I went to church and I told my pastor that God called me to preach. Here's how the conversation went:

Me: Pastor, God told me to tell you He called me to preach.

Pastor: "Oh, He did?"

Me: "Yes, He told me years ago, and now He came back and told me to tell you."

Pastor: "Well, you got to make sure God called you."

This confused me. I said, "Oh, okay."

I went back to God, and I told Him, "Well she did not say anything. So, since she did not say anything. I am not saying it any more." I kept on going. I told her again after a year or two went by, when I was told again by God, "Go back and tell your pastor, go back and tell her I called you to preach." I felt, well, I told her the first time and I do not think she believes me. And she made me question myself whether this was really God talking to me. He said, "Go back and tell her." He didn't have to keep telling me too many times. I went back and told her again. I told her, "I know I told you a couple of years ago, but God told me to come back and tell you, you know, He called me to preach. Now why has He called me to preach? I do not know. But I know He called me to preach." She sat up and she looked me in my face and said, "You tell me exactly what He said to you."

I told her when I had the vision and all that transpired, and how He told me to go tell my pastor. She patted me on my arm and said, "Okay, alright, keep praying." So I said okay. As soon as I told her, things started shifting in my life; trials and tribulations began to escalate. Then God was calling me to leave, not my church organization, but that church location.

This was something that I had never experienced. I never dealt with anything like this; I did not know what to expect. But I knew He told me to go. He told me to go and work under another Bishop in New York. She was the Bishop of the diocese of the downstate New York. The base church for me was in Freeport, New York, where she was the pastor.

I started communicating with her to tell her what God told me and to do the transition. It was not easy; I experienced a lot of bumps in the road to move my membership from my current church to the new one, but we got past that stage and began to work together. I told the Bishop that I wanted to learn, I wanted to be taught, to sit under her and glean. But this new leader I was sitting under did not like to prolong things. Once I told her, she was ready to go. Well, I was coming from a location where my previous leader liked it when people took their time to grow, to marinate, to learn and all of that, so when I was sitting down there, I did not realize that all that time I was sitting and learning. I thought I was sitting and dwindling away because I barely did anything.

When I got under this other leadership it became like an accelerated class. It was like, "I will teach you one time then it will be time for you to go forth." I was not prepared for that. And that brought its own challenges and its struggles. I told my now pastor what God told me about preaching when He told me to tell her and what I told my previous pastor when He

84

told me to tell her. She reached out to her to discuss it as she was still the chief overseer of the whole organization. The two spoke and soon after I went on to do what God told me to do.

I was able to do my first sermon in Freeport, New York, on a Friday night to an audience of five or so people. My mom, my nephew, the pastor, her daughter, and a few more people. The church did not have a lot of members. From there, our pastor continued to use me in various programs and to preach at times. But I was scared. I felt like a baby standing in front of a lot of people and not knowing the right words to say. I felt like, oh my God, I might wet myself. I was so nervous because standing behind that podium did something. It brought a level of humility that I'd never felt before. There was a level of fear. Some people say that is a good thing. I know I can speak. I know I could talk. But when I get behind that podium or I stand before God's people, that's when the fear comes. I don't see how people who preach and teach, start doing things the way they want without conviction. It was a time of accountability for me.

When I was in my local church with a minimal amount of people that was one thing, but now, I would be preaching at state conventions. This meant that my previous pastor and the congregation that I left would be there as well, and I was on the program to preach. I had to get myself prayed up. I got myself together and went up on stage to deliver the Word.

However, when I opened my mouth, nothing came out for the first few minutes, I became fearful, but then all of a sudden, the words started to flow out of my mouth. It was as if another person had taken over my body. In my mind, I kept asking, "What is this?" Ever since then I've been preaching. Since 2014.

I do not go around publicizing that I am a minister of the gospel, not that I am ashamed of it. I just believe I don't have to do that. I feel that when people encounter me, there should be an impact. People should see something in me. I'm coming from the place where I had to deal with church people who always wanted to tell you what you should look like, what you should exhibit and all that, and I was not planning on forcing my views down anyone's throat. It should be easier for someone to identify Christ in me, not just hear it from me.

So even to this day, I don't go around broadcasting who I am because I feel like I'm just an instrument. There are some people who like to announce that they are ministers, but I'm so grateful that the Lord counted me worthy, I'm still trying to wrap my head around that. "God, You called me worthy?" Eventually, the relationship with the new pastor started to sour. It was time for me to go, my season was up. I had to go back home as they would say, in the church. I had to return to my previous church location, and this was hard because I felt like my transition there to the other different location wasn't handled the best. Now I have to return to my previous pastor, who did not want me to leave in the first place, but I fought it because I felt like God told me to leave.

I have no doubt, and believe to this day, that God had told me to leave because there was a certain level that I had to learn at, and serving under the Bishop was definitely a different level of learning. I had to get to know certain things outside of my home church. Doing this built my confidence and my strength in God. I will never forget how dealing with that Bishop had me feeling like my back was against the wall at times. When I was dealing with this, the Spirit of God came and reminded me of 1 Peter 2:25, "For ye were as sheep going astray; but are now returned unto the Shepherd and Bishop of your souls." So, in other words, she could say how much she was the Bishop in the natural world all she wanted, but Jesus said, "I am the Shepherd and the Bishop of your soul," which gave me so much strength. It gave me the strength to stand. I have never been the same since.

As a child when one would leave home thinking they were grown; they would come back and eat their words. This is normal because as a parent when you see danger or something that's not the best for your children or someone else in your life, you try to help them not to go in that way without disclosing everything. Why? Half the time you just want to protect them from what's down the road, even when they are strong-willed. It felt like that. I was strong-willed, so my pastor had to let it go because I was determined that this is what God wanted and I'm going to do it.

I was so determined, though I felt like I was not given the best opportunity with the transition. It made me a little angry that all of that happened instead of the leader saying, "You know what? I'll give you a year or two or just give it some time, but I'm going to do what God said." So I was still in New York but was going back and forth to visit my old church. I'll never forget the day when my mother said, "Bev, you gonna have to just come on back because things aren't going to be right officially until you do." I said, "Mom, I can't do that, I can't go back to that church, mom. I can't do it." She began to share with me some experiences she had as a leader and decisions she had to make that made things drastically turn for the good.

She too had made decisions in her life where she had left a location because of different experiences, but then realized that she had to return even if she did not want to. I broke down and gave in. It was painful for me physically. I felt like a failure, because when I left, I had the expectation that I was going to grow, and I was going to see it. That I was going to do great things because I felt like the person I was going to serve under was able to cultivate that. And when things did not work out in that way and I had to go back home, I felt like a failure. I felt like a loser. I was expressing this to my mother and she told me that was the enemy and my flesh talking. "You cannot let your flesh tell you that." Eventually, I stopped making those declarations and requested a meeting to speak with my former pastor. I told her what happened and informed her that I was coming back. She listened and then told me about the process to return to membership.

One thing you must know about that pastor: I love her dearly but just know, she does everything by the book, by protocol, and according to the Word of God. So I had to request a new member form from the office, sign and return it, in order for my return to be official. When she told me that, I felt like, wow, okay. Anyway, I did it though I thought it was going to be handled like regular administrative activity. One day I attended church, and of course we were having a good time in the Lord, when the pastor's daughter stood up and said, "We have to make an announcement." She proceeded, "Church, we want to announce that Exhorter Beverly Davis is now back at this location as a member; she is no longer in the diocese of New York."

I felt like, "Oh my God, why?" I had to sit there and eat it up, and remember what David in the Bible said. He said, "It was good that I was afflicted" because that was how they'll know what it takes to break this flesh. Even if it does not feel good or look good, it'll be good. I would never have been able to get to the understanding and get to the level I am in Christ Jesus now knowing His Word and knowing Him personally. So, yes it was good that I was afflicted, and for me to come back home, and since then I have been flourishing. God has been prospering and using me and I mean, just using me to do His work.

I was still encountering trials that began to escalate, but I was now stronger and not easily swayed. I could go through more, without crying as much. I could now turn down my plate more, I was now quicker to ask God for His help and not keep things to myself and take it to the Lord and pray and leave it there. Being called is not an easy feat; now I am having to preach in front of the same people who once saw me fight. The same people who saw me get aggressive and talk back to others, now I get to preach to them. What can I say? It was like going through a metamorphosis and I know I had to do it on a consistent basis. I cannot put up a front. I was never a person who knew how to act that way.

God began to govern my character and govern my spirit. It was something I had to go through; the governance of my spirit and character had to go through the fire. It was God who was allowing people to test me to see what I am made of. That's when you know how big your God is, and how powerful He is. My encouragement for you if you are facing a similar situation or being mistreated, is that you must do as the scripture says and heap coals of fire on your enemy's head. Things that are supernatural cannot be dealt with using natural tools. I know it all too well. I know who the enemy is; he uses people to stand in front of you to obstruct you. It's not your family, it's not work, it is not your friends, it is the enemy. That is why Jesus is fighting for you. He told Peter, "I have prayed that your faith does not fail." He did not say, "Peter, I prayed that you will not fail. We are humans and we will fail." So, there were times when I felt like Peter, when Jesus prophesied to him and told him, "Upon this rock, I will build my church."

When Jesus asked His disciples, "Who do you say that I am?" His disciples went on to say what everybody else thought; they gossiped among themselves about what others were saying. But He said, "No, who do you say, not people?" He made it personal, and then Peter began to say, "You are the Christ, the Son of the Living God." And He responded, "Peter, flesh and blood did not reveal this to you. But my Father, which is in heaven, it is He who has given this to you, I want you to build My church and the gates of hell will not prevail against it." And that is why I felt like I was going through all those various moments; it was personal.

By now, my daughter is in college, I am a mother and a minister, still going to church with a family I cannot get along with; we cannot get along with one another. All of this is going on, and now God began to stir up the gift in me. I loved my family; I didn't feel hate but I was numb towards them. I had unresolved pain and feelings of dislike that I didn't deal with.

But God brought someone in my life who kept telling me, "Bev, you have to care for your family." I told him that I don't care for them because they don't care for me. He began to tell me some things that went on with him and his family's upbringing. Well, I thought, my family had issues. He then said, "And I had to forgive my father for abusing me and my children. I helped get my father saved." All I could do was sit there with my mouth open saying, "Wow, how could you have done that?" He said, "Because of the love of God and the power of God." This was so unreal, like, are you serious? So, he began to work with me and kept talking to me about how to deal with a particular sibling of mine. At the time I felt like she was the worst, but she wasn't; neither is she now. That is how the enemy works. My friend told me to talk to my sister and make peace. I didn't want to; I would get angry.

A perfect example of how my spirit would stir against my family is this: One day, a surprise party was planned for my mother and I wasn't invited. At first it didn't bother me because I'm used to not doing anything with my family. I was visiting one of our sister churches and needed some items I promised to help them sell after the church service. One of the elders who lived in the area rode with me to the store to get what I needed. When the elder got in the car, unknowingly he said, "Oh, I'm going to see you at the party soon." I proceeded to open up to him, before telling him I wouldn't be there, citing that my family and I do not deal with one another like that. He straight up checked me. He was like, "What? This is what the enemy wants, it's times like this you prove that you really have the Holy Ghost. you have to work things out like this." In my mind I was saying, "Sir, I need you to calm down, this is not your business." I was just so perturbed. He kept talking, stating, "No, this is what the power of the Holy Ghost is for." I was hearing him, but I was angered because I did not want to hear all that. I felt he was making his statements based on what he was hearing, but he needed more facts.

When he got home, he texted me "I pray that I will see you there." I immediately started to ignore him because I was still angry. I actually wanted to tell him off, just like I would have done in the past. He didn't know who he was talking to; I was not his child. But my spirit would not let me go there with this elder; instead, I just told him to pray for me because this was hard. We continued to text back and forth for hours until one o'clock in the morning. He wasn't hearing me; he just kept telling me what "God" told him to tell me. After we said our good nights, I stayed up and I cried the whole night. I reached out to the person who came into my life as a confidante and told him what transpired, only to hear him say, "You know, Bev, he's right, you've got to do this. You have to make yourself do this. You cannot count on anyone to do it for you. And if you wait to do it, it may never happen. You have to force yourself." I felt like everybody was forcing me, then all of a sudden out of the blue, my mother called me and said, "Your sister would like to talk to you, can you call her?" I tried to call her, but when she didn't pick up, my first response was, "She wants somebody to chase her and I'm not doing that."

My mom called me again, this time close to her birthday, asking if I had called my sister. I immediately told her, "I am not calling her; if she wants me, she can call me," and she needed to stay out of it. She responded, "Okay." She turned around and gave my sister my number. My sister called me, and we began to talk about why I wasn't invited to my mother's party. She poured out her heart, and I felt she was authentic and truthful. And that was the turning point for me, where I felt like she was being considerate. I still had my reservations about her, so I told her I had my day planned so if I could get to the party, I would get there. In the end, I decided to attend. I knew I was going to go so that my mom could see my face. I love my mom, and this was about her, not about me or my sister. I got there late, and I left early, but the important thing was that I went to the event. My sister kept wanting to take pictures with all the family and with me. I took one or two, but I was not willing to go further because we really did not have a relationship and had not really dealt with our issues, and so I did not want to sit there being fake. I told her I wasn't taking any more pictures and when I explained to her the next day at church, that I wasn't going to be fake or a phony, she understood my point.

That Sunday our pastor made an altar call for prayer. She kept saying it was not going to be a regular prayer; she was about to lay hands on folks who come up. In no time I saw a line of people going up to the altar. Sitting on the front row, I sat there until something told me to go up. It took a lot out of me because I felt the need to protect my heart. When I went to kneel, all I could do was cry out; I was crying out to God, "Oh Jesus." This was another breakthrough in my life. As I was there crying, I felt hands placed on my head. I felt my knees sinking to the ground. I said, "God, if this is what You want from me, then I surrender." When I tried to open my eyes, the pastor was putting her hand on my sister. At that moment I only wanted God to continue to restore us as a family; I wanted to bridge the gap and stop trying to be strong. It was time to let it go. I had to learn to let God fight my battles. I had to learn to let God take care of it. And I did not know how to do it without feeling inferior.

As I got up from the altar I said to my sister, "I love you, but we have to talk; we cannot walk away like this, and not talk about why we got to the place of not speaking." It was such a breakthrough moment for us; we hugged, said our apologies, and decided to drop our guards so healing could take place. We walked out of there as different individuals; I know I did. I walked out with a clear mindset that I can at least talk to my sister. Now I can smile with my sister, and I am so grateful. The same sister that I couldn't care less for earlier.

Now I was seeing what my friend was saying. It was not about what people did or were doing to me, I was not seeing the impact of my ways and he helped me realize it was on both sides. God told me He had a special calling on my life, so I had to get it right. Even if they never get it right, I had to. Sometimes, it would feel like it was not fair for Him to call me to accountability but be okay with them not getting the same accountability. But God never said He was okay with it, He just said that I cannot stay there because I was holding myself back. I could not understand it then like I understand it now. It was still a work in progress that only God could do.

God has always been calling me to a higher level, but God does not work out of order and I am learning that. He's helping me to get there; God can change things. If you allow the work to work in you, isn't it something how God can change your perspective and your outlook, even about how you view you? I never once thought that an enemy could turn into a friend but it happened with the help of Jesus. God has changed my life completely. I am not saying that I am perfect, but I am going to reach perfection in everything God had ordained for me, according to His will.

Chapter 7

ROAD TO ENTREPRENEURSHIP

I remember God telling me to write down the names of books and various things. He started telling me different things to write down, events that occurred in 2018, and before 2018. He had given me the vision of trauma, and how to help people who struggle with it like I struggled with being an underprivileged, pregnant teen, then mother. Life and things of that nature. I started to look over my life and saw where I could have benefited from that type of help had it been available.

I wanted to own a boutique. He had told me about the boutique and how He would use the boutique to help women to dress for interviews and to give them confidence. Again, because where I came from, no one did this, I didn't have those things. I did not know what business attire versus regular attire was. I only knew what church attire was and what non-church attire looked like. So, my assignment was to set up a boutique that would be more than clothes; it would be ministry and empowerment. I was supposed to have a physical location so that I could bring in speakers and build up different individuals. He just was outlining this to me step by step.

I wrote down everything I heard in the Spirit. I began to put things together and then I left it there because again, I was a starter, not a finisher. I did not know He was giving me goals to accomplish so that piece by piece I would go back and then put them all together. So, in 2018, I was at home when God began to tell me, "I want you to write a book. You are going to write a book." And He gave me the title of the first and the second one. In my spirit, I said, 'Okay, well let me start speaking my story." I didn't realize that it was in 2018 that He gave me the idea and I started to write the book,

In those two years, we had a new managing director on the job. My knowledge of submission and different types of leadership style had increased. I was stirred up back to the Word of God. Then the COVID -19 pandemic hit in 2020. God was stirring me up about getting the business started, not just the boutique, but other businesses too. Businesses that are going to eventually come into fruition as I am working on them. I said, "God all this and I don't know anybody?" And then the people I thought I knew at that time were saying they weren't trying to help or connect anyone to me. So, I would go to a place called The Marketplace in Burlington, New Jersey, and I would buy inventory from vendors there. They were nice things! I didn't care about the costs because my mother always taught us that quality was better than quantity. It will last for years. So, I was spending hundreds of dollars in that market. Until one day Victoria Swanson, a friend I grew up with in church, who now had her business in the same place, saw me. My grandmother actually knew her mother. I didn't know my grandmother, but my mother always told me about Elder Robinson having a relationship with my father's mother. So I stopped by Vicki's store; she saw me and said, "Bev, what are you doing up here, spending your money again? You know you can open your own clothing store." God had already told me that too. My daughter was grown by then so I didn't have anyone to look after or to prevent me from making this move.

I gradually started to put things together until I had everything I needed. Every time I went to The Marketplace, I would try to avoid Vicki, but she would always spot me and say, "Bev you better stop spending your money with those people and open your own clothing store." I got in my car that night and said, "God, I really could do something like this."

One day I spent a couple of thousand dollars with one vendor at the location. I had to go back to get something from him when I turned, and I saw this beautiful fur piece that I wanted. He told me he wanted a thousand dollars for it, it was beautiful! So, I tried to negotiate the price with him. "Well, I have always spent money with you, is there something you can work out with me, because right now I'm standing her with $500 to $600 worth of clothing in my hand. And these are not regular clothes, these are clothes I am buying for my convocations and assemblies and special events," I said. "I support you because I want to look nice when I go to church," I continued. But he insisted that I pay the full price; I ended up putting everything back, leaving out just one outfit. He was shocked that I put all but one back. I went over to Vicki and told her about what happened. She said, "That's your sign girl, go open your own space."

I agreed with her, considering how the guy hurt my feelings. As much as I supported his business, giving him and his wife my money, he couldn't work out a deal for me. I started putting things in motion to start my business on the side. I had been doing business for a while in my profession, so I was familiar with how to inquire, research, and get the right questions answered so that I can conduct myself professionally and efficiently.

I started to put everything together to start the business – all the necessary paperwork, my financials, and my team. My boutique, Beverly Ann's Boutique, was about to be opened! I started online, because the process of scouting around for a physical location was way before the pandemic hit, but it was proving to be challenging, and it was taking a toll on me. My daughter kept asking why I was allowing myself to be worn out. I had already started buying inventory, started getting into the swing of things We put the paperwork in, in February for an opening in July, despite feeling overwhelmed.

One thing that I have learned with dealing with God is if God has ordained something, it will not be hard. It will not be difficult. It would not come so convoluted with all these different complications. If it does, then that is something I am trying to make happen. So, I had to regroup and get myself together. And my daughter said, "Mom, why don't you start off online? A lot of successful people start their businesses online as there's a minimum amount of money required, and you get to direct it, how you need it and grow it from that point, then go from there." Though she hit it on the head, my daughter, being the smart little girl she is, I didn't want to listen to her. I said, "No, I want to be in a space because my vision is big." It was too "big" to start online. I had run myself ragged trying to figure things out until I said, "You know what? I think I'm going to start online."

However, I didn't know where to begin., I started expressing the thoughts that I don't know about starting online and inquired what I should do, but as I laid on my couch and started looking at the TV I pulled up my Facebook page and here comes Vicki. What I did not tell you was that Vicki is a very resourceful person and you don't have to ask her for a resource, she'll just give it to you.

I never asked Vicky for a thing, yet she inboxed me the info for a business coach and consultant. She said to me, "Bev, check this lady out, she's thorough and she's really bad (bad meaning good). Check her out, I know you are trying to start your business, get with her and get the help you need." So, I started checking her out and researching her. I was pleased with what I saw her doing, though I was fearful a little bit, but I knew what is going on with me. I had to make myself trust her. So as time progressed, I reached out to her for a consultation.

We connected with our consultation and I told her my goals and what I wanted to achieve, but before I ended that conversation, I told her how I felt; I didn't feel comfortable or confident in this endeavor because I had never made a move like this before. I was honest, in telling her everything – what I could and could not do. She began to tell me how she understood, and she never judged me or said anything hurtful. I could tell she was a believer by the way she acted and responded, even without seeing or knowing me prior to our conversation. This was definitely a jump for me, so she began to coach me and to help me feel comfortable, but I still was reluctant to bring her on as a coach because this was big, I had never put out money like this for something of this magnitude.

I was just getting out of the frame of mind to stop spending on clothes, and now I was just supposed to give somebody new $500 to be my coach. Somebody I didn't know anything about, was she even real? I had no idea what coaching was all about, and I just started sobbing. The old doubt, fear, and all the negativity crept up on me again. But the Spirit said to me, "Get up." Even though I had the money, I was still hesitant to bring her on board or to deal with her, but eventually I pushed past my inhibitions and took her on as my coach. As time went on, I realized I was growing, I was learning, she was teaching me a lot. She was coaching me, showing me the business. I was asking and drilling, and she was responding and setting up files, tabs, and, behind the scenes, cases, showing me vendors, putting my website together, my Instagram. I'm telling you, I was overjoyed for launch day to come. My daughter walked in the room, and she said "Mom, you went straight CEO mode on us."

I had papers and pictures everywhere. This was happening, my daughter kept saying, "You are the CEO, I will not bother you." I was like, "Yeah, I got a deadline, Joan told me to do this and that." I did everything she told me to do. I trusted that if she said it would work, it was definitely going to work, and sure enough, everything began to work during the pandemic. I was threatened with losing my job. Everybody at work was starting to get furloughed or laid off. And when I got a call from my director that it could possibly happen to me in our department, I instantly got upset, like dear Lord! I knew it was not personal, but it was still disturbing, I started to appreciate my job more. It is still unbelievable that I am now an entrepreneur, a businesswoman.

I have my own business; wow this is crazy! I could not do this over the umpteen years when others were trying to get me to do it. Then I had to come to the realization that I had to stop looking for all these other resources and connections and people to connect myself to. I have the source – God. He is my source to my resources, and He started with Coach Joan Wright-Good, a woman who is a coach, a businessperson, and a believer. I never dealt with people in business who were believers. My sentiment was never to do business with family or church people, it had to be someone from outside of church circles. I also said I was not doing any business with Black men, because it always gets complicated. Black people cannot be on time, they do business very poorly, and they play games.

My experience with the white man was, "You will get just what you want with no frustrations or hassle, but for top dollar. " So that was my theory. That was my way of thinking. But dealing with Coach Joan changed that.

We worked together well as believers; it was like family. She did not even know that she had ideas I am sure that had changed my mind about a lot. Because how I got started in the beginning was not how I ended. She made things realistic, practical, wise, and spiritual. I remember her telling me, "You're going to fulfill the vision God gave you, but you have to start off small." So, starting online was the ultimate thing to do and then it started to grow.

Things started to work out. At first, I didn't see any buyers, and I started praying, asking God to send the buyers to purchase, and almost immediately I started getting a lot of people purchasing. One person would purchase so much jewelry, up to $600 worth. The business officially took off, and then God was saying, "I had given you the vision to help underprivileged people and people where you came from, especially the youth and adults who have low self-esteem, who look down on themselves. Those who do not have the same opportunities as you have."

I didn't know where to connect. I didn't have the necessary tools readily available to me or accessible to me, but now I had a way out. He began to say, "As things begin to progress, this is how you should do it. Your birthday is coming up, what do you want to do for yourself?" And a photoshoot came to my mind. So I said, "Well, I'd like to do a photoshoot, I've lost weight and I'm doing good and feeling good. I would like to celebrate myself and I want to do it with a photoshoot." So I reached out and found someone to do the photoshoot for me. This was going to bring out the next part of this vision, which was Beverly Ann's Creations. I launched it on September 11, 2020, my birthday. Through Beverly Ann's Creations, I wanted to work with underprivileged youth and adults to help build their self-esteem, self-awareness, and self-confidence, which would bring better behavioral outcomes and life outcomes. I am still working in the same department, at work, but things have drastically changed. When the pandemic came and the killing of George Floyd occurred, it brought the point home, because we were seeing so many killings, police brutality, and other inequalities that changed the world from what we once knew.

The killing of George did something. It brought people together, not just in the United States, but from other countries, uniting us in the cause, it touched so many hearts. Breonna's death, social unrest, and injustice stirred up so much in me, and hearing my daughter's testimony about how she felt as a young Black woman working in corporate America made it worse. She had graduated from Howard University and was working at a Fortune 500 company. But she was telling me how she feels from that perspective and growing up seeing the things that were going on in the community. I began to talk to God about everything; He had been working in my life, and as I was praying, I got called into a conference call meeting with the department and the department head chair. In the meeting they kept saying, "We're going through social unrest." I began to become annoyed. So when he opened the floor asking us to tell him what we thought, everybody was quiet, especially the Black people, I seized the opportunity.

I went on to tell him that I felt very overwhelmed as a Black person; I was going through a lot of emotions, sometimes numb, sometimes anxious, sometimes anger. There was a huge pause. Then he said, "Okay, Bev, thank you, and we hope, you know, we are going to try to work through this the best way as possible." That was not what I had planned to say. I said it because I wanted to say something because everyone was quiet, and that was what came out. It was an open conference call. When I hung up, I became even more irritated and started to cry, I was very upset because I felt like they were not understanding the perils transpiring within the Black community.

People were demoralizing us as Blacks. He was not Black; he wouldn't know what it feels like. He does not know what we're going through, and up to this point, I was encouraging everybody. I had to talk to my mom, my daughter, and my neighbors. I was now experiencing what my daughter was going through. She insisted, "No, mom, this is not right. People are not even having conversations with me at the job that I work with; this is bad." Just a few days ago I was telling her, "Girl, calm down, it's your job, you got to keep your job." I was trying to help her. I was not getting it, but now I experienced it.

I reached out to my pastor because she is older and wiser. I connected with her and I told her the ordeal of the conversation and what was said and how I felt. She said, "Well, you thought you were stronger, now you have to keep praying and asking God to keep you strong." My mom also advised me to do what the pastor said. "You keep praying," she said, "but when you finish praying, you go call that man, because he does not understand the magnitude of how you feel."

After I prayed, I called him. I did not get him immediately, but I left him a message. When he got the message, he called me, and I went over what happened in the meeting. When I got finished talking to him, he said, "Bev I am so sorry. I did not understand the magnitude of my statement. I'm a minority but I'm not African American. That's why I need to learn, because neither me nor my white colleagues know how to address this issue." He continued, "Would you do me a favor? Can you, if I hold another meeting and call everybody together, would you do what you just did for me?" I said, "What's that?" He said,

"What you just said." I said, "Okay, I can try." He told me he'll be putting another meeting together, gave me the date, but when it got close, he got kind of fidgety because he did not know how it would be received. He asked how we were going to do it, so I gave him an outline – just a general outline of how the meeting would go because the Spirit told me not to tell him exactly what I was going to say.

So, the day of the meeting arrived. He came on and we had over 80 people including top leaders of the organization, and all the doctors, not just at our main campus, but throughout the network. He started off the meeting by reporting the reason for the meeting and how what he said in the last meeting affected me, leading me to call him to have an educated discussion. He gave me the floor. The Holy Ghost had me up the night before, putting something together. Ironically, as I was typing that night, all of a sudden it started storming so bad in my area. I experience storms all the time since living in Philly, but no storm like that one. It started pouring down and lightening so bad that it knocked off all the lights in the whole area.

The lightening was coming through the window, trying to hit me. I had to change where I was sitting and went to a table where I started typing on my computer. As soon as was I finished typing the lights came on. So, when I got up for the meeting, when he said, "I yield the floor to Bev," I was ready. I read what God had given me, finished, and gave the floor back to him. That was such an important moment in the conference. So many Black people began to speak up and say how they felt.

But even more white people began to ask, "How can we help?" We didn't know. This became the beginning of not just an educational moment but a healing moment. A bridge to relationship mending. Because people were coming to work, working with people who were not even acknowledging what was going on. Things were getting out of hand, which affected work productivity. People were scared to leave their homes, scared that their children would be murdered by those they trust to protect them. This was the reality for us, Blacks in America. I was pleased when the doctor in question said, "Well, Beverly Davis is our leader. You get to know her right now because she is our leader." I said, "Oh my goodness." Another doctor spoke up and said, "That's why it's imperative that we go out and vote for Biden because he is going to stop all of this mess. I wish my family were here to hear this. And I wish I had other friends and colleagues to hear it. Beverly, I have never met you, but I'm coming down there to meet you."

The next day I received an overwhelming response of emails, calls, and text messages from people who never even acknowledged me before, and coworkers started to get respectful. Now that things started to change, we started coming up with initiatives. Things we could do at work to help our Black colleagues and other minorities feel included, feel safe, and feel secure.

So now they started doing things at a higher level because we could only do things at the department level. When the meeting happened, we all started to network on all levels. My boss saw me and said, "Bev, I don't know who made you ever feel that your voice didn't matter. Whoever made you feel that your voice was not good enough; that was a lie from the pit of hell. You are a powerful woman of God, when you spoke, you kept their attention and changed the whole atmosphere." I replied, "That had to be God because He put those words together." This changed the dynamics of certain people's behaviors. They started seeing me differently; they saw that I was more than just a billing coordinator. It almost made me feel like I was having a David and Goliath moment. Nobody knew who David was, even the man who came to anoint him to be the next King. He did not know who David was. It was David's father, Jessie, who let him know where David was.

David was anointed and still had to take care of sheep but his whole life changed the day he fought Goliath. The world knew David then. He had been out there with those sheep learning God's way. I want to encourage you, when folks leave you, when they despise you and do not deal with you, don't be mad, because that gift that God gave you will work for you. Where you are coming from is a place of refinement. David used what he had; he wasn't a soldier who had weapons but he had his slingshot. I am going to use what God has given me. God gave me my voice and the vision of a boutique. I am putting them both together. Now Beverly Ann's Creations will be doing community work and conferences, to start reaching out to people who need help.

I am finishing grad school with my master's in public health in 2021. I volunteer with the Medical Reserve Corps of Philadelphia, which partners with Department of Public Health agencies. I did not know all of this was coming down the pipeline. When I told God I wanted to get my degree in public health, He knew this time was coming. He knew it would be a benefit for the church and to His people. I remember a time when I asked God about marriage, but He said, "Bev, you have come to me and I haven't forgotten you in this area. I want you to focus on school for the next couple of years." That is all He kept saying, stay focused on school, finish school. Then came the pandemic. Now I am interning with the Philadelphia District Attorney's Office. My goal is to ultimately reach the United States government and have a leadership position in Congress to help change policies on a legislative level. I could have started anywhere. And I thought I was going to start through the Department of Public Health, medical condition side. No, He had me to start with the DA. The project that I am specifically working on allows me to meet with CEOs and community leaders to help bridge inner-city communities and people to better resources.

These people do not know I'm in the ministry. These people do not know I'm in church or a believer. They are only looking on the professional side and the academics, but this is all a setup by God. Now we are at the point where I am now an author. When I spoke to my publisher at JWG Publishing House in Boca Raton, Florida, and she ran over the logistics and the cost, the breakdown for everything, I spoke to God and He said, "Bev do it." And I replied, "I know God, You got me to this point. I know all that, but it is leading to thousands of dollars now."

Things were worked out, which allowed my recordings to be transcribed into print, and now you are reading my first book.

Ministry was still happening, a family member passed unexpectedly, so I had to deal with the funeral. Then I had to help another friend who needed help with his mother's funeral. They asked me to come and do a prayer of comfort at the funeral. I got there and the funeral director came to me. She told me that they have no minister and proceeded to ask if I could prepare to give the sermon? I said, "What do you mean you don't have a minister?" And she said, "Well, I am going to call the minister that normally works with us but if, for whatever reason, he cannot come, can you put something together?" So I started to put some scriptures together that God gave me. I never did this outside of my church; I was only present for the role to pray and to support the family. She came to me to tell me that the Reverend couldn't come. He did offer to reach out to someone. But she kept insisting that she needed me to prepare.

I began to call upon God as I tried to keep myself looking calm and collected externally. But internally I was running around crazy; I called on the name of Jesus some more. I needed God first to help me keep calm. I wanted to calm my spirit so I could do this, I told Him, "God, if this is Your will, give me the words to say, bring the scriptures to my remembrance because my mind started to go blank." Then the Spirit said, "Talk about the love of Jesus, talk about Jesus's love towards men, you know enough about Him. and what He has done." That is exactly what I did. When the service ended people started coming up to me saying, "Oh my goodness you touched me. You helped me." One young lady started crying on my shoulder. I was told later that night that the family didn't get along, that people didn't get along for years, but they got together that night. Parents started getting together, spouses started getting together, friends who had not dealt with each other for years started forgiving each other. I know that that was the power of God. And to this day, I do not know all that God is calling me to do. He has not given me the picture of everything,

But I know when He leads me He guides me into all truth. I like being used by God and I understand the trials that come with it. But I also know that He said He has given us the power over the enemy. There is no good thing that He would keep from us. We can tread on scorpions and serpents and nothing will hurt us by any means.

He has given me a confidence that drives me that sometimes I cannot even articulate; only He knows. He has given me insights and vision. And He has given me so much understanding. There is no other God to me, above my God and that is why I give Him glory, praise, and worship. It makes me feel good to be a worshiper of our Lord and Savior Jesus Christ. It makes me feel good to bow down on my knees and pray to God, My Father. It makes me feel good to have the Holy Ghost. When He moves in me, it empowers me, not just in church because the churches are closed right now but at my home, in my car, and even in the bathroom. The Bible speaks about how God makes all things new at the appointed time. This is my appointed time.

Chapter 8

GOD'S LOVE OPENED DOORS

I am now coming into the realization that I have lived in survival mode for a great deal of my life. I do not feel like I was living. I feel that I was merely existing, but I thank God for where I am right now. I feel totally fulfilled in life. I finally feel happy. I finally feel grounded, not just in my personal life, but in my spiritual life with God. I am more mature and have grown so much. This could have only come through the Spirit of God, knowing God's Word, and knowing the truth of and the power of His Holy Spirit.

It brings clarity. It brings understanding through revelation on a more profound level, on a level where I do not look for people, places, and things to make me happy. I do not look for people, places, or things to make me feel fulfilled or make me feel like I am somebody. I know that I am somebody in Christ Jesus. When He said, "You are fearfully and wonderfully made; marvelous are your works," He was saying that about me.

I will not allow anyone to disturb my peace. I would not allow them to disturb my joy. I will not allow them to disturb my happiness. Any goals that I want to reach I can. I am proud of what God has allowed me to see in myself. Proud about Beverly Ann's Creations and Beverly Ann's Boutique. The boutique is not just about clothing; it helps young Black women coming from underprivileged communities who do not know how it feels to be confidently dressed for interviews and other important events. That is what I aspire to do. To bring them into an atmosphere of mentoring and coaching through the creations to help build their mindset; not only their skillset, but their mindset, because everything starts in the mind. Success does not start when you get a degree, or when you get that job, it starts in your mind, and how you see yourself.

And that is what I want to be. I want to be an inspiration, an encourager, and a motivator to these young people, as well as older ones who think less of themselves, who think their time has passed. I want to be a resource to them. I want to connect them to other resources. If it is mental health resources that are needed, I want to bring therapy to them. If it is professional or occupational skills, housing, banking, or otherwise, then likewise. We have to build them up spiritually as well, but we must be strategic in how we do it because everyone does not understand God on certain levels. Everyone does not know how to understand God, and we must learn to listen to God when trying to reach others.

God is my everything. I love and honor Him. Now I have His well to draw from. This is a new beginning for me. I cannot do anything without Christ Jesus. I am now growing in humility. And it makes me want to surrender more to him. I thank God that my sister took the time to pray with me that day before making a rash decision while I was upset. I thank God for my parents because the best thing they could have ever done was to introduce me to God, to Jesus, and the Holy Ghost.

These are the key things that I treasure. They are essential for life. Yes, they were very important for me to teach and to introduce to my child. And I hope that she does it to her children when she has them. I feel like I am just starting to live. And I am just excited and hopeful about where we are going next, and what is going to happen in my life next. I know that I am an overcomer; things I thought were going to be so challenging that I could never overcome, I did. I am understanding what forgiveness is. He taught me how important this is to my life; I feel good inside. Not based off external things like I once thought. I used to think I had to be married, keep thinking once I get married, then I will do this and do that. I thought, I had to have a certain status. All I needed was Christ.

So, this is the end of the first book, because there are many to come, He's given me so much to talk about. I hope you enjoyed reading about my journey. I hope God inspires something in you. I hope you experience growth, because that is important when looking at yourself. And waiting for God to transition your life.

www.ingramcontent.com/pod-product-compliance
Lightning Source LLC
Chambersburg PA
CBHW072201090426
42740CB00012B/2348